American Evil

The Psychology of Serial Killers

Dr Eric Cullen

☵ WATERSIDE PRESS

American Evil: The Psychology of Serial Killers
Dr Eric Cullen

ISBN 978-1-909976-79-5 (Paperback)
ISBN 978-1-910979-97-6 (Epub ebook)
ISBN 978-1-910979-98-3 (Adobe ebook)

Cover design © 2020 Waterside Press by www.gibgob.com

Main UK distributor Gardners Books, 1 Whittle Drive, Eastbourne, East Sussex, BN23 6QH. Tel: +44 (0)1323 521777; sales@gardners.com; www.gardners.com

North American distribution Ingram Book Company, One Ingram Blvd, La Vergne, TN 37086, USA. Tel: (+1) 615 793 5000; inquiry@ingramcontent.com

Cataloguing-In-Publication Data A catalogue record for this book can be obtained from the British Library.

Ebook *American Evil: The Psychology of Serial Killers* is available as an ebook and to subscribers of Ebrary, Ebsco, Myilibrary and Dawsonera.

Published 2020 by
Waterside Press Ltd
Sherfield Gables, Sherfield on Loddon,
Hook, Hampshire, RG27 0JG.

Online catalogue WatersidePress.co.uk

Table of Contents

Publisher's note   *viii*

Acknowledgements   *ix*

About the author   *x*

Introduction..xi

The Perfect Storm   *xi*

1   **The Demographics of Death**.. 15

First principle   *15*

How serial killers are made   *16*

Serial killer facts   *17*

Some basic statistics   *18*

Family abuse and fragmentation   *19*

Mental, physical and emotional isolation and abuse   *21*

A culture of violence   *23*

Violence as entertainment   *23*

Guns   *24*

Whatever happened to right and wrong?   *25*

Where does a conscience come from?   *26*

Pervasive pornography   *27*

Marginalisation   *29*

Alienation   *30*

Serial killers as celebrities   *30*

Addiction to drugs and alcohol   *31*

The biggest prison industry in the world   *32*

Disconnected and, at times, incompetent, police   *33*

Summary   *33*

The flip side   *35*

2   **Serial Killers' Personalities**..39

How it begins   *39*

Infancy and childhood   *41*

Dissociative identity disorder   *42*

Immorality   *45*

Rejection   *46*

Psychopathy   *46*

The trigger event   *48*

Psychological theories   *51*

The psychology of killing by strangulation   *51*

Diminished responsibility   *52*

Some personal characteristics shared by many serial killers   *55*

Summary   *58*

3   **John Wayne Gacy: Gay Killer Clown**... 61

When being queer was dangerous.   *62*

Positive and negative traits   *64*

Significant events   *65*

An orgy of killings … and missed opportunities   *68*

In conclusion   *70*

4   **Israel Keyes: Thrill Killer**..75

Keyes' suicide "poem"   *76*

Crucial triggers   *79*

How did Keyes become this monster?   *81*

Untypical mistakes   *83*

Motive: "Why not?"   *84*

5   **Samuel Little: The Worst American Serial Killer**...............................89

Little's story   *91*

From Samuel Little's own mouth   *93*

No conventional conscience   *95*

Psychology of Samuel Little   *96*

6   **Robert Black: The Depraved** 101

    Childhood   *101*

    An "isolated incident"   *104*

    Escalating offending and missed opportunities   *104*

    Black's psychology   *106*

    Rationalisation   *108*

7   **Michael Bruce Ross: Feeling More Real** 111

    Formative years and events   *111*

    Escalation and returning drives   *113*

    Progression to serial offending   *114*

    This serial killer's thinking and psychology   *115*

    Excuses, distortion and false compassion   *117*

    Killing as a logical next step   *122*

    In conclusion   *123*

8   **Levi Bellfield: Hiding in Plain Sight** 127

    Childhood and youth   *128*

    Impact of early experiences   *129*

    Significant factors and signals   *130*

    Staging posts and missed opportunities   *132*

    Psychology   *133*

9   **Aileen Wournos: A Prostitute's Revenge** 137

    Love and betrayal   *139*

    Seven victims   *140*

    Imprisonment   *141*

    A cultural post-mortem   *142*

    Popular culture   *143*

10 **Paul Bernardo and Karla Homolka: A Couple in Canada** 147

    Bernardo's formative influences   *148*

    Karla Homolka   *149*

    Attempts to arrest and prosecute   *153*

    Cynical exploitation   *154*

The psychology of Bernardo and Homolka   *155*

11   **Stephen Griffiths: The Crossbow Cannibal** 159
An unusual killer   *159*
Upbringing and progression to violent offending   *160*
University and more violent behaviour   *162*
Ven Pariah "Bloodbath Artist"   *165*

12   **Gary Ridgway: The Green River Killer** 169
Ridgeway's upbringing   *169*
Sexual obsession and promiscuity   *170*
Psychology of a serial killer   *172*

13   **Ted Bundy: For the Last Time** 177
Why is Bundy so popular?   *177*
"Bundymania"   *178*
Commercialisation   *179*
The psychology of Ted Bundy: "poster boy"   *180*

14   **Conclusions** 183
Human nature   *183*
Factors to emphasise   *184*
What can be done to address the fact of American serial
killing?   *185*
Humanism and secular morality   *186*
Laws against extreme, violent pornography   *187*
A nationally integrated police computer system for identifying
possible serial killing patterns and monitoring them   *188*
Introduction of new laws addressing parental abuse   *189*
Introduction of nationally funded courses in social
morality   *190*
And, finally, introduction of laws limiting the possession of
guns, and a national obligation to hand in existing guns in
private ownership   *191*
In summary   *192*

Selected References   *193*

Index   *195*

Publisher's note

The text, views and opinions in this book are those of the author entirely and not necessarily shared by the publisher. Whilst every care has been taken to ensure factual accuracy, readers should draw their own conclusions concerning the possibility of alternative accounts, descriptions, points of view, interpretations, use of terminology or explanations.

Acknowledgements

There are two people I must thank in particular. Without them, this book wouldn't have been written.

The first is Professor David Wilson. David is a charming and persuasive man and through his TV work one of the UK's best-known criminologists. Due to his exhortations, I made three series on serial killers for Monster Films which met with some success and gave me the foundations for this book.

The second person is David Howard, the Director/Producer of Monster Films. David is a former barrister, and now filmmaker, a proud Welshman. Following the three TV series by Monster Films mentioned above, I offered an extended monologue to camera on my trenchant views about America's culpability for serial killing. He suggested I write a book and get it off my chest. This is it. Thank you, David.

My publisher, Bryan Gibson, also a former barrister, has been invaluable in patiently and expertly transforming my sprawling and clearly imperfect manuscript into, well, the best he could. Waterside Press, his publishing house, frequently publishes academic works. Not a description that fits neatly on this one but I have tried to give some sources for my views and included *Selected References* at the end. So, I am doubly indebted to him for publishing it.

Eric Cullen
June 2020

About the author

Dr Eric Cullen was born in Kentucky, USA. After immigrating to England he became a British citizen and worked in borstals and other penal establishments, including Grendon Underwood (the UK's ground-breaking therapeutic community (TC) prison). Later, he worked in the private sector, notably as lead consultant for Premier Prisons Ltd in their successful bid to build and run a new 200-bed TC for offenders at Dovegate Prison in Staffordshire which opened in 2001.

He has served as a magistrate, been a government advisor and written widely on related themes of murder, life imprisonment, treating personality disordered offenders, and TCs. He contributed to three acclaimed TV series including *Voice of a Serial Killer, Voice of a Killer* (both CBS Reality) and *Making a Monster* (Sky Crime + Investigation).

He lives with his wife in Buckinghamshire.

Introduction

The Perfect Storm

I wrote this book because I was drawn into the sordid and terrible world of serial killers when I was invited to be a consultant to a television series entitled *The Voice of a Serial Killer*. I have also worked with killers, including serial killers, for over 20 years in my role as a prison psychologist and been an advisor to government as described overleaf on how to treat dangerous personality disordered offenders. Since then, I've contributed to three TV series and have, reluctantly, learned a great deal more about serial killing. What I've read has left me so profoundly moved by inescapable conclusions about how serial killers are made that I have written this book about my thoughts, findings and conclusions.

Serial killers, and the programmes, films and books about them, are a growth industry, a crowded field. It seems the public, or a sizeable section of it, find the subject morbidly fascinating. My hope is to add to the understanding of this phenomenon rather than prurience.

My main purpose is to put forward the argument that serial killers are one of several malign human by-products of a dysfunctional modern permissive society; and to show that the overwhelming majority of serial killers are the result of how significant numbers of Americans choose to live their lives. To do so I have set-out what I see as the causative elements in American modern life that lead to the creation of serial killers.

Before doing so I should outline briefly my professional experience which I believe qualifies me to speak as I do. In my career, I spent 22 years as a prison psychologist directly involved with treating offenders. I was Head of Psychology at HM Prison Grendon Underwood for nearly ten years. Grendon is a therapeutic community (TC) secure prison for the treatment of severe personality disordered offenders. Most of the prison population of Grendon are murderers. I was directly responsible for the assessment, treatment and evaluation of hundreds of these men. During my time working there, I was also a Wing Therapist for a community of up to 40 residents (inmates) and 12 staff, including psychiatrist, probation officer and prison officers. The work was entirely focused on an unrelenting, intensive therapeutic scrutiny of residents lives, their crimes and their defences, admissions, rationalisations and denials. I was also called upon on a number of occasions, both before and during Grendon, to interview serial killers.

At no time during that ten years of therapy did anyone in the institution — the most famous therapeutic prison in Europe — ever argue that any of the men there had or was suffering from a mental-illness which either mitigated or expiated their culpability. The therapy at Grendon involved staff in obliging residents to take individual and collective responsibility for their past and present acts. I know of no comparable treatment of serious and dangerous prisoners which approaches this level of scrutiny. The average time spent in therapy at Grendon was over two years and research established that, for those who were in therapy for at least 18 months, it was significantly related to reduced offending after release.

I was also an advisor for some years to the Justice Department of the Home Office of England and Wales and later following its creation the Ministry of Justice, as a member of the Correctional Services Advice and Accreditation Panel (CSAPP) until 2014. My brief was to advise the government on treatment efficacy and innovation, with particular reference to personality disordered offenders and therapeutic regimes.

I have subsequently undertaken rigorous and extensive research into serial killing, both using the internet and as an external reader at the Bodleian Library, University of Oxford. This book is the fruit of that work.

Dr Eric Cullen
June 2020

CHAPTER ONE
THE DEMOGRAPHICS OF DEATH

The Demographics of Death

First principle

S erial killers are made, not born. *The overwhelming majority of serial killers are made in the United States of America.* This book is an indictment in the form of an extended polemic based on facts, professional knowledge, experience and personal conclusions forged over many years as a forensic clinical practitioner. The simple fact upon which much of my argument is based is that the USA has only 4.25% of the world's population yet over two thirds of all the world's known serial killers to date. I believe this is a direct result of the environment in which they are raised.

Among the most salient toxic aspects of this environment is the growth of deviant, permissive and *subjective* standards for a lifestyle based on personal gratification free from cultural proscriptions or moral absolutes. In the name of liberal enlightenment, those institutions which previously offered or imposed standards of behaviour for the masses have had their influence eroded or abandoned entirely. For large sections of the population of the USA, the commandments of the church are gone, and they have been replaced by hedonistic self-indulgence. Serial killers are the malign human effluence of this dysfunctional and degenerate American sub-culture. I argue that there are clear and explainable factors which contribute to this malaise, and that these factors exist, grow and are sustained in an American environment far more than in that of any other country. Serial killing is an American phenomenon and other countries produce serial killers (in far rarer frequency) to the extent their cultures mirror the American template.

It is essential however to explain that, in arguing that the development of serial killers is predominantly a consequence of the formative influences in their lives, it is ultimately the personal responsibility of every serial killer for his or her own behaviour. No mitigation short of severe mental breakdown diminishes that burden of culpability, and even then, it would have to be closely and compellingly argued.

How serial killers are made

People who kill other people are relatively common. People who kill several other people over a period of time, often years, are statistically speaking very, very rare. The most thorough, authoritative attempt to quantify world totals of serial killers is the Radford University Serial Killer Information Center's research project, updated in April 2016. This study used the Federal Bureau of Investigation's accepted definition of serial killing, i.e. "The unlawful killing of two or more victims by the same offender, in separate events". It recorded a total of 4,743 serial killers in the world since 1900. This is a tiny percentage of the total number of people who have been born since then, approximately ten billion, so less than one in 210 million.

Is it reassuring to know that it is extremely unlikely you will be the victim of a serial killer? They are a tiny minority of the world's population, yet they seem to occupy an extraordinarily disproportionate amount of public attention. Who are these "monsters", these purveyors of evil? Where do they come from? How are they made? This book is about finding answers to these questions, and the answers are difficult to accept. As I have already indicated, I believe serial killers are made, not born. There are no people with the genetic predisposition to become a serial killer — although we all have the genetic potential to kill. Serial killers are failures. They are frequently bitter losers and should not be publicised as anything else. They are guilty of the most horrific crimes purely for malign, retributive and self-gratifying reasons.

Having worked with killers for over 20 years and been involved with and studied serial offenders as described in the *Introduction,* the overwhelming conclusion I have reached is that these offenders are the product of a number of identifiable social/cultural/environmental causative factors. And, most significantly, these factors are found in one country in far greater concentration and intensity than in any other. And that country is the *United States of America,* the country in which I was born and raised and from which I emigrated to England many years ago.

Serial killer facts

The USA has only 4.25% of the world's population, but it has over 68% of all known serial killers since 1900. By contrast, India and China, with nearly 40% of the people in the world between them (nearly ten times more than the USA), have had only 3.2% of serial killers (over 20 times fewer). This staggering difference is impossible to simply explain away, though some American apologists have tried, by suggesting it is because America is far more advanced technologically and therefore keeps better records, or that it is such a large country, with so many people, that it is not in fact over-represented. This level of superficial ignorance does nothing to obviate the obvious. All the countries of Europe, with a combined total population greater than the USA, have a far lower total of serial killers, and I would assert, technology for data collection at least as advanced as in the USA and in some European countries probably better.

By way of comparison, the United Kingdom, with the second highest total of 166 serial killers on record, which is 3.5% of the total, while over-represented in terms of its population, comes nowhere near the American total and over-representation. Put another way, the USA, with just over 4% of the world's population, has more than double the number of serial killers in history compared to the rest of the world. This statistic is so significant there can only be one conclusion. There are so many American serial killers because they are born and raised in America, and the most likely explanation as to why this has happened has to begin with a review of what it is like growing-up and living in modern-day America.

Some basic statistics

Courtesy of the National Centre for the Analysis of Violent Crime (NCAVC) in the FBI Academy, US Department of Justice:

- 93% of serial killers are male
- 75% of their victims were female
- 80% of victims are between the ages of 15 and 45
- Serial killer "motivation": sex 81.5%; profit 5%; anger 3.1%; mental-illness 1.3%; other 5.6%; unknown 3.5%
- Offender/victim relationship: customer (engaged in prostitution) 41.5%; stranger 31.5%; acquaintance 12%; "targeted stranger" 11.7%
- Psychiatric history: 32.6% of the serial killers had a prior diagnosis of psychiatric disorder, with 43% of these being personality disorder, 19% psychotic, 12% developmental disorder and 11% mood disorder
- 24% of all serial killers had a history of alcohol or drug abuse
- Cause of death: strangulation 42.5%; blunt force trauma 16.3%; stabbing 13%; gun 13%.

It is striking that most serial killers in this study were classified as having been motivated by sex, and given most of their victims were females, so many of these were prostitutes. This truly tragic fact brings home the terrible risks that being a prostitute carries in America. It is reasonable to speculate that it was not just the circumstances of risk which created this statistic, e.g. prostitutes carrying-out their profession in far more isolated, private and vulnerable settings than other citizens, but also that they are the victims of a cultural stigma which argues that they are somehow of less value as people, and that the killers would see them as the personification of those qualities or positions of power which most neuter and infuriate them, i.e. the experience is based on a woman having what a man wants and cannot obtain without buying. Hence, the prostitute is in the more powerful position whilst being in what no doubt the killer sees as a lower social status position to himself.

Any serious consideration of understanding the psychology of how a serial killer comes to be by focusing only on their personal, individual biology and character tells significantly less than half the story and is concentrating on the effects rather than the causes. I say again, serial killers are *the malign waste product of a dysfunctional environment, a cultural effluent*. There are in America today cancerous and growing areas which are landscapes of moral turpitude, sexual degeneration and permissive violence. These sprawling vistas are characterised by miles of neon and cement, no churches, few homes, no cultural centres. Inner cities in many parts of America are virtual no-go areas where even the police only patrol fully-armed and in cars, rarely venturing out on foot: slums where drugs and violence are endemic and attitudes to police and the law are hostile and contemptuous.

I was born and raised in America. I have travelled extensively in the USA and have, for this book, researched those aspects of the large and growing national sub-culture which, I will argue, provide all the influences for making serial killers. The expression which best summarises this is *pervasive cultural crapulence*. It is possible to drive for miles through cultural and moral wastelands. It is essential to detail and scrutinise this phenomenon to better understand why, as I argue, this is the petri dish for creating serial killers.

Family abuse and fragmentation

Having a family provides essential formative experiences. Your parents have an obligation to raise you in love. They protect, feed and nurture you when you are at your most vulnerable. The formative first years require stability and the reassurance that you are safe. What are the consequences when family fails to provide these essentials, when instead the child sees violence, sees a parent disappear, sees parents arguing and blaming, sees that it, life, isn't safe? Worst of all, experiences parents who abuse? In fact, it can be a hostile, frightening place.

It is, of course, better to have one loving caring parent than two at war, unstable or abusive. But I would argue that the ideal is to have two loving stable parents. For decades now, the rate of divorce in America has increased. It now stands at over 40% and will no doubt continue to climb. America has the third highest divorce rate in the world. Also, fewer couples marry at all than ever before, and unmarried couples tend to stay together less often than married couples. As a result, there are more and more children being raised in either single parent homes, or in domestic circumstances where there is a male adult present who is not related to the child, and in many instances those relationships will not be good ones.

In these fractured homes, while many may be safe, stable and nurturing, many more will not. Marripedia under "Effects of Family Structure on Crime" (see http://marripedia.org/effects_of_family_structure_on_crime) records the following findings (paraphrased):

- Over the past 50 years, the rise in violent crime parallels the rise in families abandoned by fathers.
- The rate of violent teenage crime corresponds with the number of families abandoned by fathers.
- The type of aggression and hostility demonstrated by a future criminal is often foreshadowed by unusual aggressiveness as early as age five or six.
- Strong parental bonds will significantly decrease the chance that the child will commit an act of violence.

Mitch Pearlstein, in *Broken Bonds: What Family Fragmentation Means for America's Future,* argues that:

"The United States has the highest family fragmentation rates in *the industrial* world. Nonmarital birth rates of the nation as a whole are 40%, with proportions dramatically higher in many communities as defined by race, ethnicity or geography. Divorce rates…are still estimated at about 40% for first marriages and 50% for second ones. Together, this fragmentation impacts millions of children …"

The developmental stages of children, and how they are affected by parental instability and abuse, are clearly set out on Marripedia (again paraphrased):

- First, the *broken family* creates conditions to predispose children to criminal activities. Fatherless families with mothers unable or unwilling to provide necessary affection, fighting and domestic violence, inadequate child supervision and discipline, and mistreatment of children are all common characteristics of broken families that also contribute to criminal activity.
- Second, children who come from these broken families tend to have *negative community experiences* to further encourage their criminal participation. For example, they tend to face rejection from other children, struggle in school, and participate in gangs.
- Ultimately, these conditions lead to *the collapse of the community*. Criminal youths tend to live in high-crime neighbourhoods. Each reinforces the other in a destructive relationship, spiralling downward into violence and social chaos.

Mental, physical and emotional isolation and abuse

For serial killers, there is another step: mental, physical and emotional isolation from others who might have prevented the final stages of their degeneration.

In traditional, more religious and conservative societies, there are longstanding and cherished extended families who are directly involved with their children and grandchildren. Generations live within miles or minutes, and the family regularly meets for meals, special occasions or just to be together. These traditions have long tendered an enormously important nurturing and safeguarding function, especially for infants and young children. In America, these ties and extended families living in proximity have long since diminished, while couples or single parents have travelled to other states or gone abroad. The effect is, in many cases, to isolate and alienate.

When a parent is alone and struggling to cope with children and earning a living along with all the other stressors and temptations of modern life, children can become vulnerable to neglect and, often, abuse. There is no question but that serial killers frequently (but not always) have histories of familial fragmentation, isolation and abuse. One of the essential functions of good parenting is to foster and nurture a sense of *conscience,* especially a social conscience, knowing right from wrong, good from bad, decent from indecent.

Children raised in criminal families will not have this. Those in family settings which reject conventional laws and standards of behaviour don't live in a vacuum. They create alternative family and community values based on every man or woman for themselves, the police are the enemy, it is clever to steal, rob and take and the principal objective is to get away with it and to profit.

Children raised in homes where there is physical and/or sexual abuse will not have any of the sense of safety and trust they need. If the lessons learned from parents, the main social conscience providers, involve criminal attitudes, contempt for the law, hostility, bitterness, antagonism, selfishness and identifying with a lawless group or sub-culture these only add to this. This is one significant step toward the risk of serial killing. Obviously, many people with these childhood experiences don't become serial killers, and this formative background is far from sufficient; nevertheless it is a significant factor in those instances where the child does grow-up to become a serial killer. What must be understood is that there is always at least one key trigger experience which transforms an isolated angry man into a potential killer, and there is often more than one factor which makes a serial killer out of a potential killer.

Of course, these social and cultural degenerative conditions exist in other countries, because they are part of a wider pattern, especially in first world, developed, affluent countries. These place self-gratification before altruism, profit before sharing, and indulgence of the senses before, and often in the complete absence of, moral values. But I assert this shift is happening to more people in more places in the USA than any other country in the world.

A culture of violence

"Many serial killers claim that a violent culture influenced them to commit murders": Wikipedia.

No-one can sensibly argue with the statement that the USA is a violent country. This violence comes in many and diverse forms: popular entertainment like films and TV programmes, the internet, pornography, guns, a militaristic mind-set, record numbers of imprisoned citizens for violent crimes, and perhaps, most significant of all, a tradition, born of revolution, of settling arguments and grievances personally, of taking matters into your own hands, without resorting to the police or courts.

The USA has more gun-related deaths per year than any other country in the world. America is the land of shoot first, don't even ask questions. Where millions of gun-toting homeowners would shoot trespassers and shoot to kill. Where disgruntled ex-employees take out their revenge by mass shootings. Where domestic arguments end in violent acts, including killing (The majority of all USA murders are domestic killings). Where there are more mass-murders in one month than in a year in any other country on Earth. Where every league table of violent indices is headed by one country—the USA. In such an environment, it comes as no surprise that serial killing is just one manifestation of this violent culture where America leads the world—and by a huge margin.

Violence as entertainment

The lines of reality in popular western cultural entertainment have long since blurred, but watching people being killed on TV (even in some children's cartoons) and in films—often killed with impunity as justified revenge—and where millions gorge on portrayals so violently excessive, with such ridiculous body counts, numbs sensibilities.

When young men grow-up seeing violence as a means to an end, and are alienated from others, it changes them. A young man becomes a greater risk to others. When this young man is then given possession of a gun, he becomes a greater risk still. Guns, and their part in the American psyche, deserve a separate chapter, even book, but I will restrain myself to speaking only of the part they play in serial killing. American films are, by a long way, the most violent.

Guns

There are more guns than people in America. There are more military strength weapons in private hands in America than in the American military. America is the most gun-obsessed nation on the planet. No other country comes close. Compared to 22 other high income nations, the US gun-related murder rate is 25 times higher. Although it has half the population of those 22 other countries combined, the US has 82% of all gun deaths, 90% of all women killed with guns, 92% of children and of young people aged 15 to 24 killed with guns. Between 1968 and 2011, nearly one-and-a-half million Americans were killed by guns. The obsession with the right to bear arms, and the irrational fear which underpins it, is a major factor in American mentality and by my estimation the single biggest contributor to serial killing.

Even if not used for the actual killings (though they were the cause of death in 13% of cases: see the FBI Academy statistics above), nearly half of American serial killers used a gun as their weapon of choice. Guns make killing easier. Guns enable cowards to kill. *Guns are the manifestation of a cultural malignancy beyond measure. And there is no solution, because millions of Americans would as soon kill you if you tried to take away their guns.*

The overwhelming majority of gun carrying Americans are law-abiding, stable individuals, but it is a simple product of numbers and statistical probability that the more people with guns the greater the risk of serial killers with guns using them to kill (or helping them to kill) people, and it is far easier to kill people with a gun than with any other weapon or method apart from bombing, which carries with it more issues of access and methodology. The ease with which someone can obtain a gun in America is frightening, and there are no effective checks on mental stability, or violent criminal records.

You can tell a lot about a country by the films it makes. If you watch Indian "Bollywood" films, they are full of romance, family and music. If you watch French films, they tend towards romance, dinner conversations, idyllic pastoral reflective scenes, with occasional gritty realistic inner-city social realism. If you watch American films, the majority are about fantasy escapism and violence, with the violence inevitably retributive, gratuitous, militaristic or all three. It doesn't take a university department of social anthropology to tell us that a steady diet of these films has a harmful effect on viewers, especially over several years. The culture of media violence with impunity permeates every public and private setting and you see it in the popular dialogue, where confrontation and threat feature just below the surface of countless petty arguments, and where grievances are often settled by recourse to a gun.

Whatever happened to right and wrong?

An extraordinary change has occurred in American moral thinking over the past few decades. Right and wrong have become subjective, situational and malleable. For example, the moral precepts of orthodox Christianity (or other faiths) are compromised or void for millions of Americans and the trend seems to be growing with each generation. It is inescapable to see this as a consequence of the decline of traditional, conservative, church-based (or other) religion and the increase in permissiveness regarding interpersonal relationships, marriage, sex, and business. It is equally obvious that this decline is on every level of American society, including I would suggest its highest reaches.

There are so far as I can tell no genuinely religious, moral serial killers. Serial killers generally create an extremely personal and individual set of standards by which to live; and where they do espouse a belief, it is inevitably at the vengeful end of the spectrum.

I have been unable to unearth a single record of a Buddhist serial killer. It is reasonable to say that among the world's religions, Buddhism's values and beliefs concerning right living, meditation, compassion and seeking enlightenment are totally antithetical to violence and killing. The only reference to serial killing is the Legend of Angulimala, who was said to have been a ferocious highwayman who killed many people and wore his victims' ears as a necklace. Angulimala's is a famous story because it was only when he encountered The Buddha on his travels that he foreswore his terrible ways and sought to attain enlightenment, thus demonstrating the healing, restorative powers of Buddhism even on a notorious serial killer.

Where does a conscience come from?

Have you ever wondered where your sense of right and wrong comes from? Of course, most of us will immediately say "Our parents, our family and, in later years, from those around us who we most respect." For centuries, it also came from the church. These formative influences were, and remain, crucial in creating a sense of values and or morality. That there are things which are simply wrong to think, and worse to do.

What would happen, however, if that process didn't happen. If your parents were not religious, not ethical, didn't believe in the rule of law, in the police. That in fact you were raised by someone who did not create a safe, nurturing home for you, but rather a place where you were exposed to hostility, obscene language, intolerance, misogyny, and, most lethal of all, abuse. Marripedia, reporting on the effects of family structure on crime, concludes:

> "The evidence of the professional literature is overwhelming: teenage behaviour has its roots in habitual deprivation of parental love and affection going back to early infancy. Future delinquents invariably have a chaotic, disintegrating family life. This frequently leads to aggression and hostility toward others outside the family."

And so, *the seeds are sown.* The more extreme the familial betrayal of the child in terms of abusive parenting, the greater the risk of violence towards others. And in the extreme, the greater the risk of killing. The quote continues: "By age six, habits of aggression and free-floating anger typically are already formed." There are recognised stages in human social development, including:

- early exposure to empathy, love and compassion
- first school years fostering a sense of communal co-operation, playing together, sharing, compromise and developing friendships

- adolescence and testing-out skill sets
- early sexual feelings and drives being tested-out
- early adulthood, with taking responsibility, finding a mate, parenting.

If, at any of these stages, the individual fails, is rejected, becomes isolated and alienated, it increases the risk of his (usually: most serial killers are male (above)) acting out in aggressive, retaliatory ways. Without the constraints of conscience, the checks, guidance and censure of those close to him, he has moved a significant step closer to our violent offender.

Pervasive pornography

What other key influences are there? The internet is ubiquitous, encroaching into every aspect of life. It has characteristics which are wonderfully suited to our potential serial killer. It has created the platform for unfettered pornography; explicit sexual acts which can be viewed in private; in secret. Watching other people copulating where they are debased sex objects viewed solely for gratification. Women subjected to the most extreme types of sexual abuse and violence, often seeming not only not to resist, but actively consenting or being abused with impunity.

When sex becomes a cultural form of entertainment, to be purchased, and promiscuity has lost its social sanction, and young men already isolated and rejected, view women or gay men with a combination of contempt, resentment, anger, and they are unsuccessful with their attempts to have relationships with women (or men as the case may be), they are a growing risk of violence towards women, especially if they are able to pejoratively objectify women as targets. Rape and worse enters the agenda.

What mental process is taking place in the mind of a potential rapist and killer? He watches explicit violent sexual attacks while on his own. He sees other men in happy, balanced relationships outside his narrow pornographic world and the resentment and sexual frustration grows. He begins to rationalise and justify his thoughts of taking a woman with or without her consent. He thinks of women who might "deserve it", especially either those who have rejected him personally, or "loose women", i.e. prostitutes. The former think they are too good for him and are seen by him as "bitches", the latter sell sex and are beneath him because they are dirty. The only thing they have in common is that they have what he wants and cannot have: sex. These women are the targets for many serial killers, as we will see in the individual cases highlighted in the following chapters.

A growing number of US states have declared the pornography epidemic a public health risk! According to the FBI's NCAVC research report into serial killers, the overwhelming majority (81.5%) of serial killers' primary motivation for killing was *sexual:*

> "Sexual was defined as a murder motivated by sex. This included any type of sexual interaction, no matter how subtle or diverse. Since the basis for sexual interest varied according to the fantasies of the offender, sexual penetration was not necessary for inclusion in the category."

Many serial killers do what they do for sex. But that doesn't begin to explain either why they feel the need to kill their victims, apart from reasoning that it reduces the risk of arrest by terminating the key witness, or why they would repeat the act knowing that it necessitates, in their mind, repeating not only the sexual act but also the subsequent killing. Perhaps it helps a bit to know that the second most frequently reported motive was *anger:*

> "Anger was defined as a motivation in which an offender killed victims based on personal pent-up hostility which was projected towards a person or group represented by the victim. The victim could have been a symbol of this hostility, or may have just been an available, vulnerable target to the offender. Included within this category were also cases where the offender was jealous or seeking revenge."

This speculative elaboration is quite helpful, as it introduces us to the need to begin to understand the monsters we are addressing, to understanding the psychology of serial killing, which is a central purpose of this book. Never accept any narrative which argues that serial killers have normal childhoods, happy families, are stable and have well-adjusted lives. Normal, happy, stable, well-adjusted, sexually satisfied men don't kill other people. Stay focused on the lives they live. Understand that they kill because they enjoy it. Most of them kill for sex, the strongest biological drive, which builds as a physical sensation until sated.

If a man is sexually frustrated, is obsessed with violent pornography, is repeatedly rejected by women and, more significantly, by women towards whom he feels superior, he becomes a greater risk of rape. If, in addition, he harbours a learned hatred of women in a generalised sense, or towards a particular category of women, especially women of low social status such as prostitutes, or women who are in vulnerable positions such as students away from home or those who have to work in isolated places, then he becomes a significantly greater risk of raping and killing. If he then watches images of women being killed by men who escape punishment, or he has succumbed to delusions of religiosity where he convinces himself that women who have sex for money or who are promiscuous in his eyes are "bitches, etc.", he may begin to have thoughts of killing which he can rationalise and justify. Thus begins the final stages in the mind of a potential serial killer.

Marginalisation

Another contributing factor in the making of America's serial killers is the ever-growing numbers of people on the margins of life, either by choice or circumstance. The homeless, vagrants, drifters, prostitutes, migrant workers, homosexuals, children, the elderly and hospital patients are all disproportionately targeted by serial killers. When families fracture, when extended families disappear, when communities lose the traditions of neighbourhood watch, friendliness, social events and church-based or similar activities, the social glue and knowledge of people at the margins becomes broken. The Centre for Crime and Justice Studies in London published an article on this aspect, "The Social Study of Serial Killers", in which it was stated:

> "These sort of crimes are significantly more likely to occur when there is a
> possible victim accessible to predation, a motivated offender, and a lack of

competent guardianship, and are targeted not only because they are more accessible, but also because their deaths are less likely to generate timely investigation or legal consequences."

Alienation

Related to marginalisation is the process of alienation whereby the individual fosters a sense of hostile distancing from those around him or her by wider society. This is often seen with serial killers and goes hand-in-hand with a sense of grievance, that they have been wronged, misunderstood, treated unfairly. Alienation leads in most cases to isolation. When a young man feels this strongly, his perspective changes to accommodate it. In other words, *we change reality to fit our prejudices.* He sees others as judging him badly. His sense of anger at the injustice grows and obliges him to distort reality more in order to find a sense of peace with this, his own, perceived victim status.

Serial killers as celebrities

I plead guilty to writing a book about serial killers. It would seem hypocritical of me to then cite mass media fascination and commercialisation of serial killing as a contributory factor. The distinction, however, is that this work is an indictment and a rebuke, making it an exception to most books, television programmes and movies on the topic.

> "By widely circulating the details of specific serial killers, the mass media establishes the 'serial killer' as a dominant cultural category…fostering a culture of celebrity. As Eggar (2002) demonstrated in his analysis of seven of the most notorious American serial killers, the majority 'seemed to enjoy their celebrity status and thrive on the attention they received.' Hence the complaint of a serial killer to local police is telling: 'How many times do I have to kill before I get a name in the paper or some national attention?'" (Braudy, 1986).

The charge of glorifying or celebrating serial killers is not universally true. The majority of responses by other countries to them is not like it is in America. Shame and contempt are the dominant themes, rather than a rush to buy the rights to the film or book. Americans are the highest consumers of books on serial killers in the world. Commercial cynicism and exploitation are particularly strong features of the commercial landscape in the USA, profit the first principle of the American psyche, and ideas of decency, modesty, restraint and censure are well down the list when the subject matter, no matter how sordid or distressing, has a high profit potential.

It is a shocking fact that serial killers receive offers of marriage from women who have never met them. This is only one manifestation of a common phenomenon in prison I have observed. Killers serving sentences of life imprisonment strike up a correspondence with women, which develops into something more serious. The women start visiting the prisoner and, in many cases, they marry. While it is easy to dismiss them as deluded, lonely women who are excited by the idea and feel safe because their new husband is in prison so they can get to know him safely long before his eventual release, it rarely happens that way. And there is a terrible risk which one would imagine is all too obvious. Yet almost without exception, the women recount how the man is transformed, full of genuine contrition and remorse, and no longer a risk.

While of course, in the UK, almost all killers will be released on life licence, and the risk to these new prison wives can be all too real, serial killers aren't released.

Addiction to drugs and alcohol

"In the USA, 130 people die every single day after overdosing on opioids … more than 400,000 lives lost over the past two decades": Editorial, D Orr, *The Independent*, 11 July 2019.

The epidemic of drug abuse sweeping America reaches and affects millions. The individual effects of chronic drug abuse include a criminal lifestyle, higher incidence of homelessness, dependency on aid services, and a weakening of supportive relationships such as partners and family ties. It is impossible to escape the fact that an epidemic of drug deaths, especially those from illegal drug use, has a destabilising effect on families, and that more and more broken families increase the risk of more and more dysfunctional children growing-up, and that from those, more potential serial killers are one step closer.

According to a US National Safety Council report of 2018, "The opioid crisis is worsening. Over 42,000 Americans died of an opioid overdose in 2016." This is out of nearly 64,000 drug overdose deaths in the USA that year. This represents an increase in one year from 52,000 drug overdose deaths in 2015, up 22% in one year. USA drug overdose deaths exceeded 70,000 in 2017, up 10% on the previous year. The report links the increase in major part to a significant growth in illicit fentanyl overdoses, a result of a trend towards illegal from legal prescriptions.

How are serial killers linked to this epidemic? Directly, by virtue of the effects drug dependency has on moral reasoning and reality-based lives, and indirectly through the effects a drug-dependent culture has on raising the number of potential victims. Drug and alcohol abuse are a feature of many serial killers lives and consistent with a profile which will be explained more fully in *Chapter Two*.

The biggest prison industry in the world

The USA has (as of 2016) a prison population of 2.3 million, which is both the highest total of any country on Earth and involves by far the highest rate of imprisonment. If we add those who were on probation or parole, which is another 4,751,400 people, we see that an extraordinary total of 6,899,000 adults were under direct correctional supervision (on parole, probation or in prison) in 2013. I will not labour the point to observe that, in America, imprisonment and punishment are big business. A significant proportion of serial killers have spent time in prison, many of them for years or with large numbers of convictions or both. I know from experience of having worked in prisons in both the USA and UK that American state and federal prisons can be brutalising, hardening and alienating places which can have a profound influence on men's personalities, including increasing the risk they will commit crimes when released, up to and including murder and, for our purposes, serial killing. We are made by our experiences. If those experiences are of violence as a necessity to survive (especially in prison), then some of us will come to the view that violence is a useful means to an end.

Disconnected and, at times, incompetent, police

There is no national police force in America. As a consequence, there are no convenient or effective arrangements for a police force in one state to investigate and pursue offenders into another state. They are separate jurisdictions. As a result, police frequently fail to recognise patterns of offending across state lines or fail to share information with other forces who may be investigating crimes with similar patterns. Serial killers can escape detection for years, with the result they can kill and kill again. This dreadful pattern is compounded where the victims' profiles are of groups of people who tend to be so marginalised or disregarded that their disappearances and deaths fail to be registered by officialdom.

Of course, it is unfair to criticise individual, local, county, state or federal police departments for the structure of the system, but it is difficult to escape the impression that when a serial killer can begin his grisly trail of horror in one state, and then move repeatedly between states and thereby repeat killing with significantly diminished risk of detection, there is an element of culpability which must rest somewhere. It is equally true that in many of the serial killer investigations, leads and witness evidence which would have seemingly led directly to the guilty party were not followed up by police investigating.

Summary

Serial killers are overwhelmingly American and most such killings occur in the USA. Serial killers are a product of their lives, not their genetics; formed by a number of key life experiences. Obviously, while many will experience one or more of these without becoming a serial killer, it is indisputable that most serial killers have experienced at least one, and usually several and that those experiences have been absolutely instrumental in their becoming the monsters they did. This is not to mitigate or diminish their individual culpability. All serial killers knew what they were doing and almost all actively pursued every device and obfuscation at their disposal to avoid arrest and justice. Tragically, many if not most succeeded for years.

The following is a not a comprehensive list of formative factors in individual lives and the burden of responsibility for killing lies entirely with the killers:

- a failure to be loved and nurtured as a child
- a history of physical and sexual abuse as a child or young person
- a personal history of family fragmentation or living with parents or providers who reject traditional, religious or societal principles and values
- exposure to a culture of violence, guns, and traditions of taking the law into your own hands
- alienation, marginalisation
- rootlessness/a transient lifestyle
- addiction to pornography
- abuse/misuse of alcohol and/or drugs
- experience of prison
- rejection, failure in sexual relationships
- the opportunity to give vent to learned feelings of impotence, inadequacy or rejection
- a realisation that, once having killed, he or she was not stopped or arrested, and that *they enjoyed the experience.*

These factors exist in other countries. They are obviously not exclusive to America. But the critical difference is that in America they are endemic, widespread and embedded in the cultural fabric of wide swathes of the country. To the extent that other, predominantly Western, affluent, countries also suffer from numbers of serial killers, e.g. the UK, this will be to the extent to which they emulate the American nightmare of violence and immorality.

It is important to also summarise some other brutally relevant statistics. The USA has:

- the highest imprisoned population (2.3 million) in the world
- the most mass shootings (31%) in the world
- the most murders by violence in the world
- the most deaths by opioid overdose in the world: More than twice that of any other country
- more guns per capita (112 for every 100 people) than anywhere else in the world; and finally
- by far the most *serial killers* (68%) in the world.

It is little short of extraordinary that there is so little said or written in America itself about this sordid phenomenon. You would think there would be congressional inquiries, think tanks or government agencies all focusing on what can be done to rescue mainstream American life from this growing subcultural cancer.

The flip side

It is worth concluding this introductory chapter by considering the flip side of my argument that serial killers are made by the lives they live. If we were all raised as Buddhist monks, spending all our lives in a closed community which showed us by living example that it is good and honourable to live a life of tolerance, reflection, love and generosity of spirit, *there would be no serial killers.*

Equally, I would argue that any loving, nurturing lifestyle, free from violence and pornography, where you have a supportive family and positive circle of friends, would be an environment with the greatest possible chance of never having a serial killer exist in your midst. How environmental, cultural and social factors help to create America's serial killers is reinforced in the next chapter, where I attempt to explain the creation of inner realities in the minds of these, arguably the most abhorrent of all human beings.

American Evil

CHAPTER TWO
SERIAL KILLERS' PERSONALITIES

Serial Killers' Personalities

How it begins

Having spent my entire professional life as an empirical psychologist, I am understandably reluctant to begin my explanation of the psychology of serial killing with a reference to Sigmund Freud, that internationally famous, sexually repressed Viennese conjurer. But regarding our basic drives, I confess he had a point. Freud posited,

> "There are only two basic drives that serve to motivate all thoughts, emotions and behaviour. These ... are, simply put, sex and aggression. Also called Eros and Thanatos, or life and death, respectively, they underlie every motivation we as humans experience."

As biological imperatives, these take some beating and, in the arena of multiple killing, they are, in my view, pre-eminent.

It is of course important to accept that humans also have instincts to protect, nurture and secure life, but I am unsure of the physiological origins of these feelings save that all animal life possesses them. It is, at the least, unlikely that our DNA would transmit digital codes, formed from countless generations, that oblige a tiny number of us to kill others to satisfy some obscure biological imperative. To the extent they are imperatives, sex is there for procreation and aggression for self-defence or a sense of territorial necessity.

I am equally unaware as well of other species which engage in serial killing of their own species, although related species are predatory in aid of food and sustenance, not an objective of humans who kill other humans. How sad, indeed how tragic, that sexual activity — seen as the essence of procreation — should become so traduced by those rare individuals who no longer see it as such but rather as solely the source of personal physical gratification; and that the objects of their sexual advances are nothing more than that, objects. Or, worse still, that they become something to be destroyed as inconsequential, objects of contempt, threats, or all three.

But serial killers don't become these aberrant monsters in isolation. When raised in a culture where sex has become entertainment and aggression is portrayed as a manifestation of potency, the values of intimacy and compassion are devalued. Large proportions of American popular culture are just such an environment. One where musclebound "heroes" mete out retribution with impunity. Where TV programmes are formatted to show semi-naked young people competing to copulate, in order to win the "prize". Sex is seen not as making love or intimacy but as just another act of aggression. The growing cultural obsession with internet sites which promulgate aggressive sex as entertainment also became a version of what is known as operant conditioning and the law of effect. Simply put, an action which has positive consequences is more likely to be repeated and an act with negative consequences less likely. If we experience a sex act as pleasurable, regardless of the reaction of the other person involved, we are more likely to repeat it. If someone rapes and enjoyed it, that increases the probability that that person will rape again.

The definition of sadism is the tendency to derive pleasure, especially sexual gratification, from inflicting pain, suffering or humiliation on others. It is caused by the repeated exposure to situations and images where inflicting pain, especially sexual pain, is seen as pleasurable. This is almost the perfect definition of abusive pornography and is sadly also all too frequently an element of X-rated films where sexual violence, including rape, is witnessed. Even more toxic are those images and stimuli which portray inflicting pain and suffering going unpunished.

These are universal principals. They can be applied to serial killing, especially if it is the culmination of a hierarchy of behaviours which began as relatively minor acts of sexual aggression. But we are getting ahead of ourselves, because the thought is father to the deed, and we need first to look at how serial killers come to have thoughts of killing which are fathers to the deed, the premeditation.

The concomitant act of murder becomes a logical afterthought, either to vent the angry frustrations of a life of rejections, or as a manifestation of a man's deep sense of inadequacy, or simply as a logically expedient act to remove a potential witness in the event of being caught. Or, indeed, all of these.

Infancy and childhood

How do some men, born in innocence, become so deranged, so repulsive, so dangerous? As explained in *Chapter One*, a child deprived of love, nurturing and security, and who experiences emotional, physical or sexual abuse instead, is permanently damaged. Small children are vulnerable. They are dependent upon their parents to protect and nurture them. The world is very large and at times frightening. The bond of love with your parent is the first, and strongest. How we form our self-image is largely based on how "significant others" appraise us. Irvin Yalom expressed this well in *The Theory and Practice of Group Psychotherapy*:

> "The self may be said to be made up of reflected appraisals. If these were chiefly derogatory, as in the case of an unwanted child who was never loved, of a child who has fallen into the hands of foster parents who have no real interest in him as a child: as I say, if the self-dynamism is made up of experience which is chiefly derogatory, it will facilitate hostile, disparaging appraisals of other people and it will entertain disparaging and hostile appraisals of itself."

Being abused, emotionally, physically or sexually, as a child, is the first and brutal betrayal and it changes everything. Being abused by a member of your own family betrays both that unique trust and the child's introduction to a safe world. Most serial killers have been so abused. What does it do to them?

Developmental psychology refers to the process of child development and of how important it is in the formation of an adult. Strong attachment to parents, especially to a mother, is the subject of more child development literature than any other. If a young boy is abused by a parent, it is usually his mother's boyfriend or stepfather rather than his biological father. What then if his mother takes the side of the abuser and thereby allows the abuse to continue? This is a primal betrayal and confirms to the child the world is unsafe, even from his mother.

If a child is abused, physically, emotionally, sexually, that child is betrayed. The first and most fundamental of trusts has been broken and the child learns lessons which will stay with him or her and, in many cases, distort their personalities, for life. They learn that being emotionally close to someone is dangerous. That trusting someone is dangerous. That committing to a relationship is dangerous. That other people can be dangerous. They, in the worst instances, learn that inflicting pain on others is better than risking having it inflicted upon themself. They associate being in control in a relationship as both safer and more powerful. These primary, often familial, early experiences define the character of the adult. What then happens at adolescence and young adulthood to compound the damage is also crucial.

Dissociative identity disorder

There is a psychological construct called dissociative identity disorder (DID), which has been coined to label behaviour which has two defining characteristics. The first is *depersonalisation*, which is feeling detached from one's own body. The second is *derealisation*, which is feeling separated from the world around us. We are told that research highlights childhood trauma and attachment difficulties as the two main causal factors in developing DID. When a child is betrayed by a parent or other caregiver, any adult in a position of power and trust who betrays that position by abusing the child, that is trauma.

If the trauma is repeated over time, the child has little option but to either:

- invest in massive psychological and emotional rationalisations, e.g. "This is an act of love, my carer is showing me affection and love"; or
- must withdraw, detach, dissociate.

Equally, when a male child is growing up and becoming sexually aware, he may experience a sexual attraction or arousal towards his mother. If the mother displays herself in sexual ways, such as appearing in her underwear or naked, it may form a significant and disturbing association in the boy or young man's mind, one of ambivalence or, in some cases, hatred and contempt towards her.

Combine this with a mother who is a prostitute. One who actually brings clients into the home and the son witnesses the sex. How might these experiences combine in the formative mind concerning his attitudes towards sex and prostitutes? Perhaps it isn't just because they are vulnerable and isolated women whose profession carries with it a strong element of danger? Perhaps serial killers often rape and then kill prostitutes because of their childhood and formative experiences.

The vital determinants of adolescence for males is their experience of sex, and how they are treated by females, especially those to whom they are attracted, and their exposure to aggression and violence, especially to an end. The unique intensity of "first love", of the attachment to, and often fixation on, a teenage girl or boy is defined by whether he is accepted or rejected. Even more vital is the nature of the rejection. So much of our sense of self-worth comes from these early encounters. So many young American boys are growing-up in broken homes, where alcohol, drugs, violence and anti-authority attitudes dominate. Some of these young boys will already have the seeds of potential to do violent harm to others within them. Some, fewer still, may already have thoughts of killing and of hatred of women and these thoughts become merged into a mind-set which equates strength with aggression and a growing belief that if he is to be successful he will have to take what he wants by whatever means he can. I posit that many serial killers are formed by the time they reach their physical sexual maturity and that all that is lacking is the trigger experience (see further below).

If the commission of an act of aggression against another person is experienced positively, in other words if he enjoyed the experience either as a sense of potency, due to the positive sensations of relief and dominance, or simply because he got away with it, then the probability he will be aggressive again is significantly increased. This fundamental learning principal is vital in our understanding of the gradual sequence of learning which leads ultimately to rape and murder. Once an inadequate young man who has felt repeated rejection and failure knows that feelings of power and control, of dominance go unpunished, he sees new opportunities which will seem, to him, positive and rewarding.

He will by this stage have already probably been viewing pornography which either portrays women as willing participants in sex, and often rough and aggressive sex where frequently there is the pretence of force, or video games where armed "heroes" routinely kill ridiculous numbers of victims with impunity. Indeed, they will be rewarded. He may, by this point in his life, have developed a habit of drinking alcohol or taking drugs, legal or otherwise. These will, when used in excess, alter his moods and disinhibit him, especially in terms of his urges and drives to have sex or be verbally or physically aggressive. He will also have gravitated towards other young men, similar to himself or, as is more likely with potential serial killers, will have isolated himself emotionally and physically. He will have cultivated an extensive inner world of thought.

This is key.

His world will be one saturated in a sense of grievance and unfairness, in which he sees himself as misunderstood and badly treated. The timebomb is now ticking. Once he has gone to a prostitute and had to pay for sex, he will see a whole group of people who he can look down on and towards whom he will feel resentment at having to pay for something others take for granted.

Serial killers are not successful in their relationships with women. Homosexual serial killers are not successful in their relationships with men. There is within them a strong drive for revenge and a need to find people towards whom they can feel superior.

I came across an interesting article entitled "America's Deadliest Serial Killers", and it referred to the 23 serial killers with the most victims.

Surprisingly, of the 23, 16 had killed prostitutes or boys/men during sexual encounters, and of these, nine were homosexual and had killed either men or boys during or after sex. That's 40% of America's worst serial killers having homosexuality as the principal factor. What to make of that? Unless we assume that roughly 40% of the adult male population of America is homosexual, which I suspect is unlikely, there is something else operating as a trigger factor.

Perhaps it is something to do with the emotional torment of accepting his sexuality in the midst of a family and a culture with homophobic values. Is it possible that killing gay victims is a manifestation of the killer's own self-hatred? Is there a short distance from the arousal and aggression of some homosexual acts and the violent release that comes from lethal aggression against those that "tempted" them? This is admittedly speculation, but it would be interesting and possibly illuminating to study the statistics on serial killers based on their sexual orientation and victim gender.

Immorality

The *Cambridge Dictionary* defines immorality as "behaviour that is morally wrong, or outside society's standards of what is acceptable." That is perfectly clear so long as we have a form of collective agreement and understanding of what we regard as morally wrong and, more crucially, that society still has standards of what is acceptable. There are large and growing areas in American society whose moral standards are so low, so compromised, that an individual who is immoral may be simply hedonistic, or liberal, or the CEO of a large multinational corporation, maybe in high office, even as president of their country.

Serial killers may have their own moral code. They may have rationalised their beliefs to accommodate their deeds. Equally, when they have been raised to either reject traditional moral values and standards, or have never been in a family or circle of friends who subscribe to these standards, they may not even see what they are doing as wrong, living as they do in a corrupt and brutal world.

Rejection

When a young man first ventures into having a serious relationship with another person, there is a sub-agenda of which they may not be aware. They will be exposing their sense of manhood, of potency, to risk of rejection. When that young man has had a life characterised by rejection and failure, and where he needs to gratify his sexual drives and his sense that he can be attractive and successful, and is then rejected or, if at once successful, he is betrayed, the consequences can become dangerous for the woman or man who is doing the rejecting or betraying. Or others on whom that danger is then visited.

Psychopathy

I must begin this section with a confession. I am dubious about the construct called psychopathy. I say this because most contributors to the crowded field of explaining serial killing will refer to psychopathy as a given. One of, if not, the key explanatory aspect. My disclaimer will be mercifully brief. I feel the use of psychopathy is a largely tautological construct which fails to add to or clarify our understanding of the reasons why men become serial killers.

The authors and champions of psychopathy label it a spectrum disorder and there is a list of 20 characteristics provided as a result of completing a questionnaire to determine whether you are a psychopath. All of these are negative/critical qualities, including pathological lying, glib charm, grandiose sense of self-worth, cunningness, manipulation, sexual promiscuity, and lack of remorse. I have been directly involved in the use of the Hare Psychopathy Checklist-Revised for many years when I was Head of Psychology in a secure psychiatric treatment prison for dangerous personality disordered offenders. The PCL-R was used as a screening tool for offenders being considered suitable or not for treatment and was often the arbiter against acceptance as it was felt they could not benefit from therapy as they could not change.

The problem with this is that: (a) everyone who undertakes the questionnaire will have a score for psychopathy, i.e. it isn't possible to have a score against, i.e. demonstrating alternative positive qualities; and (b) there has to be a cut-off score where the assessor labels someone as either psychopathic or not, yet the scores are by definition on a numerical continuum, so I could score 30 and be labelled a psychopath, but 29 and not be. You may think this insignificant, but in the USA, a high score on the PCL-R for a prisoner could significantly influence whether he is released.

This test has incredible power in the American criminal justice system. "It's used to make decisions such as what kind of sentence a criminal gets and whether an inmate is released on parole. It has even been used to help decide whether someone should be put to death" (Alix Spiegel, npr 24-hour program stream, May 26, 2011).

In an article in the *Journal of Psychiatry and Law* (29(4) 433-481, December 2001), J F Edans stated:

> "Psychopathy has gained increasing importance in the field of risk assessment in the last decade, in large part because of the established association between this construct and future violence and criminality…one recent application of psychopathy has been its inclusion in death penalty cases, wherein PCL-R scores have been introduced to support the position that a defendant will represent a 'continuing threat' to society-even if serving a life sentence in prison. Despite such claims, a review of the relevant research indicates that the empirical basis for these conclusions is minimal at present."

What this reveals is that decisions about imprisonment, freedom, life and death are being made on the basis of a pencil and paper questionnaire which is based on an hypothesis — a series of verbal constructs designed to establish the extent to which individuals describe themselves as possessing pre-determined characteristics. Depending on how they tick the boxes, they might be signing their own death warrant!

The second edition of the *Hare Psychopathy Manual* avows there are many "non-criminal psychopaths" in history, including Winston Churchill. I am lost for words. While I could perhaps start to understand citing current American President Donald Trump as a psychopath, such a specious assertion about the "greatest Briton of all time", and arguably one of the greatest and most principled statesmen of this or any generation, is to my mind beneath contempt. We will return to this question later in the chapter, but it's time for me to say what factors *are* relevant to our better understanding of serial killers and how they are made, in the context of the characteristics outlined above.

It is true that many serial killers show an obvious indifference towards the emotions of their victims, and also that many of the characteristics of the PCL-R are ones which we can see in them as well. Do we then conclude that serial killers, like psychopaths, are incapable of change? After the fact of their serial killing you might agree with me that it no longer greatly matters and that the question is whether all serial killers have forfeited their right to release (some would say to live at all) and that issues of rehabilitation are irrelevant. However, what does matter is whether or not we might identify potential serial killers and, having done so, could there be interventions which could substantively alter the risk they pose? It would presumably be agreed that if this were possible, then it would unquestionably be worth doing.

The problem with using the psychopathy construct as if it were proven and definitive is that, as with some American prison systems, it can then be used to determine the life or death of prisoners by virtue of precluding the potential for positive change. If I were a prisoner who had killed and I indicated I was at risk of killing again if released should I then be put to death? Labelling a serial killer as a psychopath does nothing to advance our understanding. It is irrelevant, both in terms of identifying potential serial killers and what sentence they should receive.

The trigger event

In order for someone to make the transition from simply being a potentially lethal killer to killing, it is necessary for him or her to think of killing, or to premeditate. This is simple enough, and I dare say some of us have been so angry with or felt so badly treated by someone to wish them dead. Of course, as soon as the vast majority of us think this, we have reproachful, self-critical thoughts that of course we don't mean it and would never do it. But not everyone is like that. However, if you are to understand the psychology of a serial killer, you must accept that humans have the potential to kill and that, given enough provocation, most and possibly all, would.

When a man has experienced one or more of the significant life experiences I've outlined so far, he is at a far greater risk of killing. While most murderers who have only one victim are not at risk of killing again, I believe a significant minority of murderers would represent such a risk if they weren't stopped after their first killing. These are men who still possess a sense of injustice, have low self-esteem and who enjoyed killing the first time. Enjoy may sound the wrong word, but believe me, having worked with hundreds of murderers in intensive individual and group therapy over many years, I know this to be the case. Serial killers however have one significant thing in common: they were never caught either the first time or during the series of murders they committed (i.e. only when captured in the end). Obviously, many of them if not arrested would have continued to kill, but the point is they got away with it!

It is easy to have the thought of killing, especially if you see your potential victims as easy and safe targets and you care nothing for them. Most serial killers' primary drive or motive is, in the first instance, rape. Not sex, rape. Once they have raped, they are at immediate risk of arrest. If, after the first rape, he kills the victim, the killer has significantly reduced the risk of arrest because, obviously, the only person who could identify him is almost always the victim, so it is simply expedient. If the killer takes pleasure in the killing, then he has been doubly reinforced (rewarded) and is more likely to kill again. We are back to Freud's two primary drives: sex and aggression.

The cumulative effects of one or several of the causative factors I've mentioned are necessary before the potential serial killer engages in the thoughts which precede the deed. Many serial killers objectify their victims, in which they dehumanise them, no longer seeing them as individuals with lives, feelings, dreams, families, etc. The killer is detached, indifferent. For others, their victims are deeply personal. But only in the sense that they are either people who the killer knows and feels a hostile and intense hatred towards, or they represent someone towards whom the killer bears a grudge or grievance, such as Ted Bundy (*Chapter*

49

Thirteen) killing so many attractive young brunette long-haired women who looked like the one he had "loved" and who had rejected him.

The serial killer Michael Bruce Ross (*Chapter Seven*) killed eight young girls/women, all of whom "were dead as soon as I saw them". Ross was a sexually frustrated deluded fantasist who said of his youngest victim, aged 14: "The smallest it was so close to the ideal, it was like a fantasy. That one bothered me the most; she was so small and co-operative." This extraordinary and chilling narrative shows us something of what we are dealing with. Ross is signalling that he still retained a conscience of sorts but that this vestigial fragment never troubled him more than to mention he was bothered. He needed small, immature, compliant young women to satisfy his sick needs. From a young age, Ross stated he would have fantasies in which he would "kidnap women and take them to my place of safety and they would fall in love with me ... James Bond sort of thing." How he could equate this pathetic inadequate depravity with the Bond male archetype simply illustrates the magnitude of his dissociative fantasies. Psychiatrists at various times said Ross was a sexual sadist, mentally-ill, mentally-disordered, suffering from psychopathology. These words label and describe; they don't explain. Ross maintained he couldn't control himself, but he selected victims and engaged in detailed and successful hiding of bodies and avoiding capture for three years.

It is typical of killers that they attempt to rationalise their behaviour in order to minimise culpability and displace blame onto others, or "uncontrollable urges". There are no uncontrollable urges, only weak people. There are no sexual addictions. Sex, and aggression, are biological drives which are satiated by physical acts. Similarly in my research, I have not found a reputable reference which persuades me that sexual sadism is anything other than a descriptive label for deviant behaviour, or that such behaviour is other than the responsibility of the individual who commits murder in this way. Failing to control these urges is indicative of a weak character, a depraved mindset, and a choice. Ross was a highly manipulative, intelligent, callous, totally self-obsessed sexual inadequate.

Another type of serial killer is the one who takes advantage of being employed in a medical setting. The most obvious examples of this are Harold Shipman, the British general medical practitioner who according to Dame Janet Smith's governmental investigation (2000-2005) put to death at least 215 of his victims, this a manifestation of both his contempt for his patients and his pathetic need to feel potent; and Elizabeth Wettlaufer, the American nurse who killed her elderly and often demented patients out of a perverted sense of compassion which gave way to killing some older men, I suspect due to her generalised bitterness towards men for a life of failed relationships and rejection. She was obese and plain and seemed to harbour bitter feelings against men. These serial killers were opportunistic in satisfying their perverted needs and bitterness, and I suggest they were unlikely to have been serial killers had they not been in positions of trust which allowed them to kill with relative impunity.

Psychological theories

Various psychological theories attempt to explain serial killers, but usually with little or no reference to socio-cultural influences. Vronsky (2004) theorised that, not only abuse during childhood, but also the relationship between serial killers and their mothers is crucial developmentally. Moesch (1998) posits that the mothers of these "monsters" tend to breed men that hate females, due to mothers who were over-controlling, over-protective, physically and/or emotionally abusive. This speculative assertion is as can be imagined not popular with feminists, who see it as just another attempt by men to blame women for their depravity.

Traditionally, theories attempting to explain serial killing have adopted one of three perspectives: biological, psychological and sociological. This is an irrational distinction. We are a product of all three, and serial killers are no exception. There are, however, several theoretical models of serial killing, and I feel obliged to mention a few: Diathesis-Stress Model, Frustration-Aggression Hypothesis, Trauma Control Model, Anomie Theory.

The psychology of killing by strangulation

The most common method of killing by serial killers is strangulation (*Chapter One*). I suggest this is best explained by understanding that, for the majority of killers, the primary motivation is sex and dominance.

It follows logically that the intimate, direct and terribly personal act of strangulation is an intrinsic part of that drive. It requires closeness. It is direct and merciless. It is the laying on of hands to malevolent, lethal purpose. It is the final act of dominance and power for a man who has lived his life in impotence.

Diminished responsibility

It is incumbent upon me, given the focus of my polemic, to deal with the question of state of mind as it pertains to serial killing. More specifically, the construct of diminished responsibility. In criminal law, it is considered that, if a defendant may be "suffering" from impaired or diminished mental functioning, defence attorneys may argue that this is grounds for either mitigation or being found not guilty by virtue of an inability to choose between right and wrong, between breaking the law and not. As I have argued that serial killers are the product of malign life experiences which are of enough magnitude, repetition or effect, do they retain the means, psychological and emotional, to choose right from wrong? Are they still substantively accountable?

According to Wikipedia, most states accept the concept as being admissible in full or partial defence in one form or another. It is interesting to note too that the concept of "irresistible impulse", a rather broader defence, may be used. It is not for me to question the place of either diminished responsibility or insanity as defence positions. They are part of the legal fabric. What I can posit however is that so long as a man or woman is not certifiably psychotic, they retain a degree of personal responsibility for their actions. In other words, in the UK, e.g. unless a court accepts psychiatric opinion that a defendant was insane at the time of the offence, and therefore not capable of understanding what they were doing, they are culpable. It is a question of an even greater principle: personal accountability.

Another weakness of the courts relying on determinations of state of mind is that the experts who pronounce on this invisible condition are psychiatrists. How do you establish empirical substance to show the presence or absence of a degree of something which is entirely the subjective creation of people with a vested interest?

The argument against, or at least for limited application, is well put by Nicholas Hallett, in *Psychiatric Evidence in Diminished Responsibility* (2018, *The Journal of Criminal Law*). He addressed the wording of the 2009 Coroners and Justice Act, regarding the role of expert psychiatric evidence, and concluded:

> "...the new Diminished Responsibility is not a purely psychiatric matter. This is because of the moral dimensions inherent in the defence, the ambiguity in the statutory wording and the fundamental problems of psychiatry usurping the function of the jury in relation to the ultimate issue. This results in inconsistent application and role confusion in relation to the defence and asks psychiatric evidence questions it cannot answer."

There are distinctions to be made between insanity, diminished responsibility and, not forgetting, "irresistible impulse".

An insanity defence is used as an excuse, arguing that the defendant is not responsible for his or her acts due to suffering from a mental illness, either temporary or persistent, at the time of his or her offences. As we are only dealing with serial killers here, and part of the definition is that the murders were committed over time, i.e. separate temporal events, then we can dismiss the temporary insanity plea. Indeed, in many serial killer cases, the acts of killing may have been carried out over many years by people who are in other respects living relatively normal, functioning lives, so again it would seem unlikely that a defence of mental illness could be successfully mounted in these cases. There have been however infamous cases such as those of Aileen Wournos (*Chapter Nine*) and Michael Bruce Ross (*Chapter Seven*) where the defence teams employed psychiatrists or psychologists who submitted evidence that these serial killers were "mentally-ill", the first (Wournos) with borderline personality disorder and the second (Ross) as a sexual sadist.

Significantly, all classifications within the DSM-4 (Diagnostic and Statistical Manual of Mental Disorders) suffer from poor inter-clinician reliability. In other words, the psychiatrists and clinical psychologists struggle to agree with a reassuringly high degree of reliability. It is worth mentioning too that they are dealing in a language which is entirely based on descriptive labelling of behaviour and that the labels are the creations of other psychiatrists in the past. If we applied their diagnostic labels to any 100 people, I would confidently predict that we would see both poor inter-rater reliability and over-use of the labels such that far more of us would be tainted with a psychiatric tag than could possibly be justified.

I confess I struggle to understand what these impulses might be and presume to suggest that, if the courts in some American states allow this as a mitigating defence, then the idea of humans being able to exercise control over their thoughts and actions is itself at risk. My view is that this concept, along with many others, is indicative of a society which seeks to minimise personal responsibility. Much of America, and for that matter, modern societies, subscribe to the "Me First" maxim, and a big and growing part of that is the myriad claims made to avoid taking responsibility.

Another example of this is the labelling of a range of self-inflicted conditions such as alcoholism and sexual promiscuity as forms of addiction. They aren't. They are forms of abuse, either to the self or to others. There is no such thing as a sex addict. There are only people who seek to excuse their compromised conduct. You might almost argue that many in America are suffering from cultural and ethical diminished responsibility. When you grow-up in an environment obsessed with self-gratification and devoid of moral imperatives, you are set upon a course of living an increasingly unprincipled life. Psychologically, you grow convinced you are no different, no worse, than people generally, and that you are simply living as you see others live. There is a self-fulfilling pattern. You learn to behave badly. To treat others as grasping and unprincipled and, therefore, not worthy of being treated respectfully. This is a descent into living down to your basest instincts and drives. Put another way, it is a variation on the classic police trilogy of motive, means and opportunity.

Some personal characteristics shared by many serial killers

While serial killers are a disparate group, defined mainly by their acts of killing, there are some aspects of their stories which many share. I will describe some of these characteristics.

- Humans live their lives balancing their inner and outer realities. We spend countless hours in our own minds, reacting, reflecting, remembering. Our realities, how we see the world around us, determines how we behave. The extent to which our reality matches the empirical reality is a good measure of how successfully we live our lives. If we see people as essentially good, if we feel safe in our world, both the very personal family and friends' world and the wider world we see through the lens of the media, then we have a more healthy attitude towards others. If we view the immediate and wider world as hostile, uncaring and ugly, we will eventually behave towards it with an unhealthy attitude towards other people. If we are so damaged by our life, or if we are so obsessed by our drives and feelings about sex and aggression that our view becomes dominated by those experiences and the feelings they create in us, then we are a short step from extreme violence towards others. When these malevolent life views cause us to withdraw from healthy relationships and the rich positive wider world, then the step is shorter still and it needs only a trigger. The trigger (also mentioned in the text above) can be something someone else says or does that affects us in a precipitative way, or it can be in our minds, a time-bomb ticking away and the fuse growing ever shorter, until we tip over into brutality. Into killing. And if we enjoy the killing, and the sex, and the torture, and we get away with it, then we will do it again—and again. Thus, is a serial killer made.
- A history of abuse, of being in a vulnerable, powerless position. From this, potential serial killers learn to associate and identify with the person in the powerful position who is able to gratify themselves, rather than with the victim. This allows both an

escape from the experience of being abused and an opportunity to take a kind of revenge.

- The absence of a conventional social conscience. Serial killers in general have conspicuously failed to acquire a sense of right and wrong towards others sufficient to act as a restraint against committing extreme harm. There is no contrition because this requires guilt and serial killers usually either failed to learn this or have long since abandoned the necessary compassion.

- A learned withdrawal and isolation. Distancing themselves from others, physically and emotionally, is a way of forming a buffer from being hurt and rejected, as well as a way of freeing the self from the influence, control and disapproval of others, sufficient to allow the potential killer to grow and nurture the nascent fantasies and rehearsals usually needed as a stage towards the deed; the act of killing. In other words, emotional detachment serves to enhance the ability to create an unchallenged inner-world of justified violence.

- Objectifying victims. Many serial killers target a specific group, like prostitutes, gay men, children and the elderly. These victims are targets for the gratification of the serial killer's extreme need for sexual gratification, and an element of the related sense of dominance, power and control. This power is also often a compensation for the reality of being relatively powerless, or a failure, in their efforts to create normal relationships. The victims are usually strangers who have the characteristics, or life-styles, which the serial killers have learned to hate.

- Victims need usually to be vulnerable, less able to defend themselves, not a threat.

- Premeditation. Most serial killers don't act solely on impulse or situational provocation. They have learned to plan in detail and to anticipate what could go wrong from their perspective and, crucially, how to avoid detection and capture. When a serial killer acts without premeditation, there is still often a subconscious drive, impulse or in some way relevant motive associated with what might be thought to be reacting to situational provocation.

- An addictive personality. Whether it is drugs, alcohol, pornography, violence, or infamy, serial killers often have a strong element of acquired dependency on some form of thought-altering addiction or obsession.
- Failure to achieve healthy, fulfilling social, interpersonal and sexual relationships. The related sense of rejection.

I believe too that for many serial killers there has been a vital shift in their thinking towards an inner-reality. Most well-adjusted people strike a balance between our inner reality, where we reflect, imagine, interpret and judge, and our outer reality, the rest of the actual world. This equilibrium is, I believe, essential for a healthy, well-adjusted life. When an imbalance develops, due to traumatic events or gradually over a lifetime of real or imagined injustice, the inner-reality takes hold, unchecked or challenged such that the individual can free himself or herself from those vital checks and balances on his or her thoughts and behaviours until he or she can think and act unconstrained. It isn't madness necessarily. It's a dysfunctional distortion.

There are many ways in which serial killers are substantively different, if occasionally overlapping with, mass-murderers or those who only kill once. Serial killers kill two or more people over time. Mass-murderers kill several people in the same temporal event. Those who only kill once, or at least the overwhelming majority of them, only kill once and in that act significantly reduce the likelihood of ever killing again because they have expiated the source of their provocation. That is, most murderers have killed someone they know, usually a wife, girlfriend or close family member. Over 90% take only one life determined by the circumstances, e.g. rejection, jealousy or revenge, and their victims were known to them because they had been in a relationship. This is not true of serial killers. The majority of them kill victims whose only relationship with their killer is commercial or predatory.

Summary

In summary, serial killers become monsters as a direct, gradual, cumulative consequence of their life experiences. Most influential among these are abuse and rejection as a child; coming from a fragmented or broken home; exposure to pornography, violence and unpunished crime as a youth and adolescent; developmental experience of enjoying impersonal, aggressive relationships and learning that dominance and control can be satisfying, rewarding and pleasurable; living in a sub-culture which is free from moral imperatives or even the experience of people who are positive role models with whom the potential killer could identify; abusing alcohol and/or drugs in order to distance and distort reality, to numb the senses and to disinhibit self-control over more base urges; moving away from family and friends; isolating themself from as many of the interpersonal, cultural and legal influences and controls as possible, and focusing on other, infamous, serial killers who might become role models, or targets to exceed in victim numbers and depravity; being rejected by a love object; having a job which permits access to vulnerable potential victims. And, most important of all, being born in a country where all these influences are there in abundance: in terms of my polemic the USA. It is simply a statistical probability that, if a far greater number of people (overwhelmingly men) have experienced enough of these toxic learning experiences in one country, then that country will ultimately experience a far higher number of serial killers as a consequence.

Once the necessary toxicity of thought is in place, the potential serial killer is in place, and all that remains is having the thought of committing the act. That thought then takes hold in the mind. It is cultivated, refined and rehearsed. It is premeditated. All then that is needed is the opportunity, and the deed is done. Once done, if the killer enjoyed it and is free to kill again, he or she will. That is the psychology of a serial killer.

What, then, of the individual cases of serial killing which give example to these causative experiences?

CHAPTER THREE
JOHN WAYNE GACY: GAY KILLER CLOWN

John Wayne Gacy: Gay Killer Clown

John Wayne Gacy was an American serial rapist and killer who raped and murdered at least 33 young men between 1972 and 1978. The tragedies of these young men's lives, taken and destroyed by a violent coward have been compounded beyond measure by allowing them to become just footnotes. I intend to clinically dissect Gacy's sordid life in order to better understand the nature of how dangerous, predatory men like him are created.

Gacy was the son of an immigrant man who is recorded as having been a violent, abusive alcoholic. The family lived in an area of Chicago, Illinois, the heart of the American Mid-west and, historically, the country's slaughterhouse. He was born in 1942, during World War II. His father was a car mechanic and World War I veteran who drank, hit his children and wife, and who named his first and only son after an American film star and cultural icon, the actor John Wayne. This is an essential starting point in understanding this serial killer.

The actor John Wayne was, for over three decades, a symbol of American masculinity: tough, swaggering, heroic, good with his fists, decent and, above all, heterosexual! He was what Gacy Sr wanted his son to become. Tragically, for many people who were the victims of this time-bomb, the son could never be what his father wanted him to be. He was short, fat, sickly (he had a heart condition) and poor at sports. He strove to gain his father's pride and approval—and failed.

But the crucial failing, one which spelt disaster and death for many innocent people, was that *John Wayne Gacy was homosexual.* It is recorded that "Gacy's mother attempted to shield her son from his father's verbal and physical abuse, yet this only succeeded in Gacy earning accusations from his father that he was a "sissy" and "Mama's boy" who would *probably grow up queer.*

When being queer was dangerous.

Being gay in Mid-west America in the 1950s and 1960s was illegal and dangerous. Then, it was called "sodomy" in the courts, and a lot worse everywhere else. Having sex with another man would cause you to be imprisoned. It was such anathema that it was often associated with anti-nationalism, i.e. it was viewed as being un-American. It was illegal in every state until (ironically) made legal in Illinois (Gacy's birthplace) in 1962.

Homosexuality was listed in the *Diagnostic and Statistical Manual of Mental Disorders* (American Psychiatric Association) as a mental illness until 1973. If you were openly gay, you could, and frequently were, beaten, and were certainly the target of jokes, ridicule and abuse. The language then was of being a "fag", or worse. If his aggressive, old-fashioned and intolerant father had discovered he was queer, he would have beaten the young Gacy and disowned him, and the rejection and humiliation would have been unbearable to the son.

What I will attempt in this, as in all these cases, is a clinical *post-mortem* of the mind and personality of the killer as it bears on his or her serial killing. Gacy had a long history of parental abuse including humiliation and punitive over-control by his father. He would have been emotionally traumatised by this but his fixation on his father and need for approval was so strong that no amount of rejection was sufficient to turn him against this abusive man, and "throughout his childhood, Gacy strove to make his stern father proud of him", always failing.

During his teenage years from age 14 to 18, Gacy was hospitalised for over a year in total without the doctors ever reaching a conclusive diagnosis. During this period, his father suspected it was all an attempt to gain sympathy and attention and accused his son of faking his condition. If, as we now know, Gacy was already aware of his homosexuality, and of how dreadful it would be if it was openly known, especially by his father, it is hardly surprising he was presenting with various undiagnosable conditions and spending time in hospital, due to either genuine ill-health or, more probably, attempts to gain his father's more supportive attention.

Gacy may have been subconsciously subscribing to the prevailing cultural view of homosexuality as an illness and placing himself in hospital in an irrational effort to find a cure. His familial history is full of incidents which would have embedded in his mind that he was a disappointment; his growing sexual identity was something different and dangerous—something to be hidden. He was attracted to boys more than girls. A terrible and perverted secret.

Already, at this stage, I suspect Gacy would be trying to distance himself from these sexual drives and attractions; to suppress them and trying desperately to foster his more heterosexual urges. It would have been impossible for Gacy to experience homosexuality as anything but abnormal, ugly and dangerous. But sex is the strongest biological imperative and, as a teenage predatory homosexual, he would have experienced intense and prolonged sexual frustration at being unable to gratify his urges with behaviour which would gain familial and societal approval. In fact, if he was caught in a homosexual act, he knew it would devastate him, his parents and family, and prospects for a "normal" successful life.

When his father's brutalising rejection finally drove Gacy from his home, he went, aged 20, to Las Vegas, an interesting choice for a young man raised in Chicago by purportedly religious-minded parents. There, he found work as a mortuary attendant. Not really, it might be thought, a job choice consistent with someone in a healthy state of mind. Young men would not normally gravitate to death and the dying when first freed from the shackles of what was clearly an unhealthy home environment.

Gacy slept behind the embalming room, observing the bodies of the dead. He later confessed that, alone one night, he got into a coffin with a teenage male, "embracing and caressing the body before experiencing a sense of shock." Why did Gacy do that? What motivated him? Is it something a normal, healthy, well-adjusted young man would do? No. This is the first recorded instance where Gacy was able to experience what I would describe as "safe sex", because I am convinced that he got into the coffin with premeditation, in order to experience intimacy consistent with his nature. I would further speculate that he was already sexually aroused beforehand, and that climbing into the coffin was in order to consummate this sick, necrophilic act. Significantly, this act alone introduced to the young Gacy a whole new world of possibilities associated with the potential for safe sex with the bodies of dead young and, preferably but not necessarily, gay men. The awful stage was set.

It would seem at least that there followed a period of a few years when Gacy was attempting to create a conventional heterosexual public life-style, acquiring a wife and two children whilst still living a double life and secretly pursuing opportunistic homosexual encounters. It is hardly surprising that he should try and build a "normal" lifestyle as his public face, even if he was already rehearsing his violent homosexual fantasies.

Positive and negative traits

The picture of this killer would be incomplete from our psychological perspective if we didn't hear more from this period. From returning home to Chicago after his abortive Las Vegas experience, Gacy seems to have made a sustained and quite successful attempt to live not only a heterosexual life, with a wife and two small children, but also to have been conspicuously successful in business and the local Chamber of Commerce. Of particular significance is a reconciliation with his father in 1966, when the latter is recorded as having proudly said, "Son, I was wrong about you."

The flip side of this positive period was that it is recorded that Gacy was simultaneously engaged in wife-swapping, pornography, prostitution and drug abuse; so a life of deception, duplicity and degradation was never far from home. I suggest this aspect of Gacy's life is significant both in illustrating that his private morality was already compromised, and that he was sexually indiscriminate.

In 1967, aged 25, Gacy sexually assaulted the son of a member of a political organization in which Gacy was also involved. The victim suffered sexual abuse from Gacy for several months before telling his father. At this point, Gacy hired one of his employees to physically assault the victim to prevent him attending Gacy's trial. This backfired, as the victim along with several other teenage boys came forward to give evidence which resulted in Gacy's first conviction; followed by a sentence of ten years in the state penitentiary for sodomy. This legal term was entirely consistent with the biblical terminology and enforcement powers that pertained under American criminal law at the time. The effects upon Gacy's wife were immediate. The day he was convicted, she filed for divorce, and he never saw her or his children again. Indeed, there is no mention of his ever attempting to see them after his conviction. We see in this the public confirmation of Gacy as homosexual and the degree of selfish obsession that excluded contact with his own children, and it must have created the unmitigated shame and sense of betrayal that his wife would have felt.

Yet, his devotion to his father endured. While Gacy was in prison, his father died one Christmas Day. When told of this he is reported to have collapsed to the floor, crying uncontrollably and having to be supported by staff. He was denied release to attend his father's funeral. Although not immediately apparent, his father dying would have freed the homosexual Gacy from much of his repressed urges.

Throughout this period, there is no mention of Gacy's relationship with his mother. Despite having been sentenced to ten years' imprisonment, he was paroled after only 18 months as he had proved extraordinarily adept at playing the part of a model prisoner. This is significant in that it evidences his cunning capacity to present as plausible and normal, a skill set which was to serve him exceedingly well in the years to follow when he indulged in his greatest depravities whilst maintaining a convincing public persona.

Significant events

Gacy was released from the prison in Iowa, and immediately broke the conditions of his parole by returning to Illinois, thus escaping both proportionate justice and his record of being a sex offender which might have been significant in subsequent attempts to identify the serial killer he was to become. He returned to Chicago and lived with his mother. There is little known about why she would have taken him back into her home given the humiliation he had brought down upon the family.

It was then that he met his future second wife. It is clear that Gacy was either bisexual or driven to present as straight whilst living a secret life of sodomy.

These were hugely significant events in the creation of Gacy as serial killer. Firstly, he had now been exposed for what he was and, although imprisoned for it and losing his wife and children, his actual punishment was extremely minor for the then seriousness of his crimes, but he no longer had to maintain the pretence of being a straight married man. His father dying also freed him from the humiliation he would have felt from his father discovering what his son was.

Even then, Gacy would continue to try and live a double life as a successful businessman, husband and father, and a man who was active in charities, dressing-up as a clown and performing—something at which he had become extremely adept. It is probable that by now he knew all this was a sham, and that he was gradually being drawn down into the depravity which had no doubt been in his mind for many years.

Gacy was paroled in June 1970. In February 1971, he was charged with a sexual assault but not convicted as the victim failed to appear at court. This coincided with his criminal records being sealed, thus freeing him from any subsequent inquiries concerning known sexual offenders.

He started "cruising", picking-up teenage boys from bus stations and other logically anonymous target areas. He claimed his first killing was unintentional. In January of 1972, he picked up 16-year-old Timothy McCoy, who was visiting Chicago, and who accepted the offer of a bed from Gacy, in all innocence. During the night, they engaged in sexual activities. The next morning, it is recorded that Gacy was in bed when he became aware of McCoy coming into the bedroom brandishing a knife. Gacy mistook his intentions and they grappled, before Gacy took the knife and stabbed the victim to death in over-reactive self-defence.

Gacy later recorded that, at the moment of killing he had "a mind-numbing orgasm", and "that's when I realised that death was the ultimate thrill." More accurately, what he was recounting was that killing a teenage boy after sex was, for him, the ultimate thrill of power, sex and release. He got away with it. This was, unquestionably, singular and of great significance in the making of this particular serial killer. *The experience was sexual, it was an act of power, conducted in secret, and crucially, it was intensely pleasurable and went unpunished. These elements are absolutely crucial in the making of John Wayne Gacy, serial killer.*

So, consistent with the pattern of creating a normal heterosexual public lifestyle while continuing to abduct, rape and murder young men, Gacy married again in 1972. He became established as a respectable member of the local community, successful businessman, active in local Chamber of Commerce events, with a wife and stepdaughter. He was also abducting, handcuffing, sexually assaulting, raping, torturing and killing innocent young men, both homosexual and heterosexual. Gacy raped and killed an unknown boy aged between 14 and 16 before burying him in the back garden of the Gacy home. I could find no information as to any police investigation of the case which refers to Gacy even being questioned.

In 1975, apparently the strain of sustaining this double life became too much for him and he told his wife he was bisexual and that they wouldn't have sex again. He is reported to have become increasingly distanced from her, and unspecified "strange" behaviour was observed by neighbours, which we might be forgiven for thinking may have been related to his killings.

He and his second wife were divorced in 1975. Now completely free to indulge his homosexual perversions, living alone and completely inte-grated into the local community with a business as a building contractor, Gacy's serial killing was unleased in full measure. In the same year, he tried to trick a young employee of his, Anthony Antonucci, aged 15, into handcuffs. Antonucci, a keen wrestler, was able to escape. But he never reported the incident to the police. However, Gacy tried the same trick on another young employee of his, John Butkovitch, aged 17, who Gacy strangled to death.

It surprises me that there are, again, no records of Gacy even having been interviewed for these crimes, despite him being their employer, having been seen regularly with the young men, and having as it tran-spired buried one of them under his house. The floodgates of his killing were now open wide and Gacy free to give full vent to his sexual power fantasies. The years that followed, 1976-78, were described by him with typical callous self-obsession as his "cruising years". In fact, only one month after his second divorce was finalised, he abducted and murdered his next victim.

An orgy of killings ... and missed opportunities

There followed an orgy of killings, most of which had the same methodology. I won't detail any of these because this book isn't about feeding the prurient; it's about explaining the deviant. Suffice to say, Gacy was now completely depraved in his savage drives for power, dominance, rape and murder. Throughout this extended period of killing, there is no indication that the police had the slightest clue as to who was committing all these horrific crimes or, indeed, that they realised they were dealing with a serial killer. It would be derelict of me not to reflect, at least briefly, on factors which allowed Gacy to kill so many for so long.

Gacy's second wife seemingly had ample reason to be suspicious of his darker lifestyle, given that she is recorded as having been told by Gacy that he was bisexual and that they would no longer be having sex. She also admitted observing Gacy bringing teenage boys into the family garage and finding gay pornography inside the house. In fact, the Gacys had agreed to a divorce as early as October 1975 but she continued to live in the family house for another four months before moving out. During this time, Gacy was actively involved in abducting, raping, garrotting and killing young men, some of whom were his employees. It strains credulity that Mrs Gacy made no connections or had no suspicions sufficient to go to the police. Also:

- Anthony Antonnucci (already mentioned above) had managed to escape Gacy's attempts to kill him, in exactly the same *modus operandi* as most of his other victims, and never reported his assault to the police
- the parents of John Butkovich (again above) "called police more than 100 times, urging them to investigate Gacy further", yet there is no record that the police did anything
- another lucky escapee, David Cram, was handcuffed and assaulted by Gacy. Cram managed to defend himself, but he was

subsequently told by Gacy that he had intended to rape him, saying, "Dave, you really don't know who I am. Maybe it would be good if you gave me what I want." Not only did Cram not think this suspicious, remembering that it happened in the middle of the three years when Gacy was killing many young men, some of whom had also worked for him, but Cram continued to work part-time for Gacy over the next two years!

- Robert Donnelly was abducted at gunpoint by Gacy, raped, tortured and nearly drowned, repeatedly. He survived and reported the assault to the police. Gacy was interviewed when he claimed he had been having "slave-sex" with Donnelly and insisted everything was consensual. The police believed him, and no charges were filed. The following month, Gacy killed again.
- Gacy used employees of his construction company to bury the bodies of his victims under his own house, and this apparently was never seen by anyone as suspicious or worthy of police investigation.
- Jeffrey Rignall was lured by Gacy into his car in 1978. This young man was chloroformed, driven to Gacy's home, where he was raped, tortured and repeatedly rendered unconscious. He was lucky in that Gacy let him live. The police were again informed of the assault but did not investigate Gacy.

Finally, Jeffrey Rignall took the matter into his own hands and, with friends, identified Gacy's car and followed him to his home address. Gacy was arrested on 15 July 1978 for a "battery" against Rignall. Then he was arrested in December for the murders. Throughout all this period of three years, there were numerous and obvious opportunities for the police to at least question Gacy concerning the missing young men, now numbering 33, if not actually arrest him. They had found no bodies. If they had obtained a search warrant for Gacy's home at any point, it is impossible they would not have uncovered the massive cemetery under the crawl space of his house. It is, to my mind, an inescapable conclusion that there must surely have been incredible and prolonged police incompetence during these years. It is for the reader to conclude as to the magnitude of culpability that appears to be implicit.

In conclusion

John Wayne Gacy was the product of 1950s machismo. In Mid-western America he had a tyrannical abusive alcoholic, rejecting father, who nonetheless Gacy loved and was desperate to make proud; and there is Gacy's conflicted hatred of his own homosexuality, which he decided he could only satisfy by raping and killing.

He was a repressed, secret, aggressive homosexual who experienced intimacy with a dead teenage boy, had an orgasm, learned to associate relationships with same sex younger vulnerable boys, was irredeemably conflicted about his sexuality throughout efforts to live a heterosexual life, and finally gave this up and committed himself to gratifying his need to rape and kill, and then to keep the bodies close — literally underneath him! He could never be the John Wayne his father would have loved him to be. He wasn't mentally-ill in terms of psychiatric language and understanding. He was devoid of any recognisable conscience. The main reasons he killed were:

- He enjoyed it. Abduction was exciting and risky, but he always got away with it (until the very end).
- Sex with young boys met his sexual drive and frustration.
- Dominance and control, being in a position to taunt and tease sex objects fed both his lifelong need to feel powerful and strong, and was a perverse manifestation of his conflicted personality wherein he was both attracted to and repelled by the same sex object.
- He had to kill his victims: the only way he could feel safe from arrest and punishment, which he knew would be execution
- He experienced the best of both worlds in that he was seen by others in his community as a successful, intelligent, colourful *heterosexual man,* at the same time as living a completely immoral alternative *homosexual killer* life which served to both

satisfy his physical and emotional needs and to be a kind of perverse revenge on the intolerant culture into which he was born and that looked down on him as a perverted *sodomite.*

Gacy was eventually caught after a remarkably extended and, to my mind, questionable investigation. Even when he became the prime suspect due to his casual incompetence in his last abduction and killing, the police failed to obtain a search warrant, relying instead on staking-out him and his house. This surveillance was further compromised it is reported by a couple of officers allowing themselves to be invited by Gacy into the house for alcohol and friendly chats!

He was eventually convicted in 1980 after it took just two hours for the jury to find him guilty. Then, thanks to the Byzantine complexity of American appeals system, he managed to live another 14 years in prison where he became famous. No, not infamous; famous. This was because he had created a clown character called Pogo or Patches, and would appear at children's parties, parades and fund-raising events and entertain them as a clown character. I attach no psychological significance to this strange pastime other than that, apparently, professional performers commented that the make-up he used had elements which made the character rather more menacing than that of traditional clowns. Gacy might well have enjoyed the cruel irony of being seen as a happy clown making children laugh at the same time as he was brutalising and killing young men, such was the depth of his secret depravity. He painted clowns. His paintings were subsequently sold for a total of approximately $100,000. This money was then given to his children, step-children and sister, thereby ensuring that not only was Gacy allowed to become a celebrity for 14 long years during which time the families of his 33 victims continued to suffer, but his relatives were able to profit from his celebrity. Why wasn't it given to the families of his victims? Why wasn't his entire estate settled in their favour?

I watched an interview of Gacy years after his conviction and shortly before his execution. You see all you need to understand concerning what a self-obsessed, callous, insensitive, contemptible and insignificant individual he was. Having confessed to his murders in open court and been found guilty, he was nonetheless, even just before his execution, protesting his innocence. The day before, he told a news reporter: "There's been eleven hardback books on me, 31 paperbacks, two screenplays, one movie, an off-Broadway play, five songs and over 5,000 articles." This is a measure of what was important to him. His last words were: "Kiss my ass". What he never realised was that he was hated and reviled in the way reserved for what seems to be the basest of life forms, the serial killer.

While it might be said that Gacy was born homosexual, what he became was entirely a product of a culture which forced him to subvert his sexuality and made him into a serial killer as a direct consequence of abrasive and rejecting parenting, growing-up in a place where he was always going to be a freak and a failure if his secret were known. He then could stay alive via a legal system which was incapable of exacting the punishment ordered by the court until many years had passed, during which he became famous and enjoyed it. That was John Wayne Gacy. Made, emphatically, in America.

CHAPTER FOUR
ISRAEL KEYES: THRILL KILLER

Israel Keyes: Thrill Killer

Israel Keyes was an American serial killer who was clever, calculating, detached, arrogant, cold-blooded, self-obsessed, brutal and trained to kill. When finally caught, he confessed to eight murders and was suspected of at least three more. Keyes would be described as a "thrill killer" as his primary motive seems to have been the thrill and challenge of successful hunting. His story is one that can only be of someone born and raised in the USA. He was a product of place and circumstance. He was made in America.

Keyes was born in 1978 in Utah. His parents were Mormons who home-schooled their four children. The family moved to the far North-west of the USA, close to the Canadian border, where they joined "The Ark", an avowedly Christian identifying sect known for its racist and anti-semitic teachings. I suspect they were typical of the seemingly perverted, extremist small collectives which America produces and which teach prejudices antithetical to true Christian or moral values. During part of this period, the family lived in a cabin without gas or electricity.

Keyes was taught self-sufficiency and survival skills. During this early period of his life, he became close friends with Chevie and Cheyne Kehoe, known racists, who were later convicted of murder and attempted murder respectively. Although raised in a purportedly Christian sect, Keyes disavowed religion as a young man and pronounced himself an atheist. This apostasy was part of the chain which eventually led to his criminal lifestyle. This is a not untypical American anti-social childhood!

In summary, Israel Keyes was influenced by parents who were counter-culture, advocated a frontier self-sufficient life, had good friends who were killers, a loss of religion, and came from a fringe sect which preached racism and anti-semitic tropes. In terms of the usual motives, Keyes seems difficult to understand; apparently a motiveless serial killer (but see further the final section of this chapter).

Keyes' suicide "poem"

There isn't an obvious sexual, financial or vengeful motivation. But if we read the letter/poem he wrote just before he took his own life in order to sustain his dominance through the last act and cheat the justice system of due process, we can see something of his mind-set. I reproduce it entire here so that I can analyse certain parts of it. It was found badly bloodstained from his own blood after he had slit his wrists and bled out.

'Where will you go, you clever little worm, if you bleed your host dry?

Back in your ride, the night is still young, streetlights push back the black in neat rows. Off to the right a graveyard appears, lines of stone, bodies moulder below. Turn away quick, bob your head to the seat, as straight through that stop sign you roll loaded truck with lights off slams into you broadside, your flesh smashed as metal explodes.

You may have been free, you loved living your lie, fate had its own scheme crushed like a bug you still die.

Soon, now, you'll join those ranks of dead or your ashes the wind will soon blow. Family and friends will shed a few tears, pretend it's off to heaven you go. But the reality is you were just bones and meat, and with your brain died also your soul.

Send the dying to wait for their death in the comfort of retirement homes. Quietly/quickly say 'it's for the best' it's best for you so their fate you'll not know. Turn a blind eye back to the screen, soak in your reality shows. Stand in front of your mirror and you preen, in a plastic castle you call home.

Land of the free, land of the lie, land of scheme Americanize! Consume what you don't need, stars you idolize, pursue what you admit is a dream, then it's American die.

Get in your big car, so you can get to work fast, on roads made of dinosaur bones. Punch in on the clock and sit on your ass, playing stupid ass games on your phone. Paper on your wall, says you got smarts. The test that you took told you so, but you would still crawl like the vermin you are, once your precious power grids blown.

Land of the free, land of the lie, land of the scheme, Americanize.

Now that I have you held tight, I will tell you a story, speak soft in your ear so you know that it's true. You're my love at first sight and though you're scared to be near me, my words penetrate your thoughts now in an intimate prelude.

I looked in your eyes, they were so dark, warm and trusting, as though you had not a worry or care. The more guiless [sic] the game the more potential to fill up those pools with your fear.

Your face framed in dark curls like a portrait, the sun shone through high-lights of red. What color I wonder, and how straight will it turn plastered back with the sweat of your blood.

Your wet lips were a promise of a secret unspoken, nervous laugh as it burst like a pulse of blood from your throat. There will be no more laughter here.

I feel your body tense up, my hand now on your shoulder, your eyes ... forget the lady called luck she does not abide near me for her powers don't extend to those who are dead.

[Illegible lines]

My pretty captive butterfly, colourful wings my hand smears…punishment and tears.

Violent metamorphosis emerge my dark moth princess…come often and worship on the alter [sic] of you flesh…You shudder…and try to shrink far from me. I'll have you tied down and begging to become my [illegible] sweetie.

Okay, talk is over, words are placid and weak. Back it with action or it all comes off cheap. Watch close while I work now, feel the electric shock of my touch, open your trembling flower, or your petals I'll crush."

When Keyes took his own life, on 2 December 2012, by cutting his wrists and strangling himself with a bedsheet, he left this under his blood-soaked body. In a Thoughtco.com profile of Keyes, they record: "An analysis of the enhanced letter concluded that it contained no evidence or clues but was merely a 'creepy' Ode to Murder, written by a serial killer who loved to kill." They further quoted another unattributed source: "The FBI concluded there was no hidden code or message in the writings. Further, it was determined that the writings do not offer any investigative clues or leads as to the identity of other possible victims."

I agree that there were no further clues relevant to a police investigation, but I disagree completely that the letter/poem tells us nothing about Keyes. This was written by a man about to take his own life. I believe it tells us so much about his killing and his contempt for conventional American life, and for life itself. There is a morbid mutant eroticism too, with tragic implications.

The first line of the "poem" is a soliloquy. Keyes is speaking to the worm within which is the serial killer his body sustains, and which he is about to bleed dry. He then lurches directly to reminiscing on his last drive across the South-western states of America before he was caught in Texas. I believe this dramatises the end of his freedom to kill, equating it to a car crash. He then, almost whimsically, reflects on his freedom and on living his lie, which was, of course, the many years of living the dual personality of successful worker with his own business, a girlfriend and daughter on the one hand, and a vicious but successful serial killer on the other. He ends it with a hard, atheistic lament. He sees himself as strong, self-sufficient and above the bovine masses, who would be but "vermin" if their comforts from the "grid" were lost.

To me, the poem is a grandiose death soliloquy, left deliberately as a final taunt to life and the authorities. Keyes was in charge of his life, and his death, and they were powerless to stop him. His deluded and distorted self-image was most significantly formed by his having been, in his own eyes, a successful serial killer. Nothing else in his life was of any significance, and he knew it.

Crucial triggers

As already noted, Keyes was raised in a cabin without electricity during part of his childhood. He chose to live in Alaska. He was independent and kept guns. He had placed himself outside conventional American life. But all of this is true of many thousands of his contemporaries who didn't, and don't, go on to kill. So what was the crucial trigger point? Keyes was reported to have admitted that when he was only around 18 or 19 he raped a young girl in Oregon. He told FBI agents that he separated the girl from her friends and raped but did not kill her. Although he confessed that he had thought of killing her and decided not to. There is no record of his having been asked why he raped the girl or why he thought of killing her and of deciding against it. But this was clearly the stage in his life when he was rehearsing the thoughts and plans for future killings. It is reasonable to assume that, now that he'd had thoughts of killing, he carried them with him as a challenge to his manhood, something concerning which he needed to prove himself.

The record then tells us that Keyes committed a long list of crimes, including burglaries and robberies, and that he was skilled at these offences; also at accumulating funds in reserves which he would subsequently draw on to pay for his extensive travels across the continent. This pattern would continue into the next century, when he added many bank robberies to his repertoire, such that he funded his killing expeditions from these rather than from his construction company.

It is clear Keyes was an unusual serial killer in several key respects:

- Firstly, his motive seems to have been more to do with being a successful hunter/killer than for the satisfaction of physical drives such as sex and aggression.
- Secondly, he was a meticulous planner and executor, both in the sense of detailing his forays and in the killing process itself. He took great pride in his murders, which he saw as an affirmation of his manhood. His typical method was to fly from his home in Alaska to a targeted part of the country, rent a car and then proceed to drive great distances to a previously targeted area for the killing, where he would have already hidden the paraphernalia of execution. He looked for remote areas or places where he would stand the best chances of both not being seen and of successful escape after the killing. As with other cases in this book, I deliberately avoid detailing his crimes and refer readers to other, more salacious and prurient works of mawkish interest. For purely factual purposes Keyes used a "killing kit" to murder by means of a gun and strangulation/asphyxiation.

In the passage in his letter/poem which begins "Send the dying to wait..." he shows us his hatred and contempt for America, and when he speaks of "Land of the free..." he shows us the depth of this contempt and, I would argue, a life lived outside that dream, one which pushed Keyes to Alaska, and isolation, and ultimately into the dark heart of death and destruction.

The next passage, beginning "Now that I have you...", I suggest Keyes is talking to his female victim, possibly the last but equally it may be a collective discourse. Although his describing the captive victim as "my love at first sight..." to express his thoughts as "penetrative" and an "intimate prelude" is obviously intended as both sexual and affirming his power over her. Dominance and submission would be, even now, an aphrodisiac to him. These chilling insights continue as he "fills up those pools with fear", referring to her eyes and his intent. This dreadful scene of the victim's final moments unfolds further with direct reference to "the sweat of your blood". This horrific passage gives us a vital insight into the mind of a sexual predator and how, for Keyes, a sexual encounter was defined by menace, threat, torture and brutality. It is essential, if we are to understand this serial killer, that we see how he thinks, how he feels and how he justifies his obscenities. Keyes was giving himself one final sexual arousal and reminiscing on his grisly history of brutal killings.

The remaining part of the letter/poem simply confirms this analysis. His "violent metamorphosis" is the culmination of his twisted and psychologically disturbed reality, where he is acting out his hatred for "soft" people and for the women he has raped and killed. He closes with words which I believe show us both his creed for killing and for his final act of arrogant defiance.

How did Keyes become this monster?

Keyes' association with the Kehoe brothers was, I speculate, a signal experience where he would have talked about violence towards others even to the point of murder. His early teenage experience of rape and the thoughts of killing his victim would have occurred at a time when he was testing himself in terms of his developing hatred of soft conventional people, and the beginning of a number of crimes he committed including burglaries and robberies in an early-stage criminal lifestyle which featured threats, violence, rape and thoughts of killing. Given Keyes' personality, these thoughts would have been relatively detailed and served as a rehearsal for later acts.

Soon afterwards, Keyes enlisted in the US Army, where he was trained to kill with guns and taught the self-discipline the military requires, without presumably the essential message to distinguish these from living a successful life after release from military duty. He was discharged in 2000 and made his way to Alaska. This would have been an ideal location for him to cultivate his nascent thoughts and plans for a life of killing. He created a network of murder kits which he buried across continental USA, including at least in Alaska, New York, Washington, Wyoming, Texas and possibly Arizona. This remarkable and, as far as we know, unique behaviour is the product of a calculating, organized, pre-meditated and deliberate murderer who intended to kill-and-kill-again, and get away with it.

The skills he obtained so expertly were entirely of the killing variety. He was awarded several decorations or awards: the Army Achievement Medal; Army Service Ribbon; Expert Infantryman Badge; Air Assault Badge, and, most significantly, *Marksman Badge with Rifle Bar.* Those who served with Keyes described him as a quiet loner who drank whisky to excess. Another soldier who knew him during active service said he was "disturbed by a dark side that sometimes surfaced." When Keyes was offended his buddy's comments included, "He'd drop his head ... knit his brow, lower his voice and say, 'I want to kill you, McGuire'."

Keyes now had the killing skills he would need in his imminent serial killing career. I suspect he had also experienced in the Army a mind-set which justified killing in the military sense but, to Keyes, it wouldn't have been a stretch to translate this, filtered through his amoral and misanthropic mind-set, as an invitation to give full vent to his darkest proclivities. He was heavily influenced, and I would suggest perhaps significantly, by his obsession with the music and personalities of his favourite music group, Insane Clown Posse. These two, who call them-selves Violent J and Shaggy 2 Dope, appeared during performances with face make-up perhaps best described as a cross between horror and clown, faces guaranteed to horrify children at least. According to Wikipedia, ICP "perform a style of hardcore hip hop known as horrorcore". Released under the Psychopathic Records label! It doesn't require a qualified psy-chologist to make sense of the influence this would have had on Keyes. Again, Wikipedia spells out:

> "The songs [of ICP] center thematically on the mythology of the Dark Carnival, a metaphoric limbo in which the lives of the dead are judged by one of several entities. The Dark Carnival is elaborated through a series of stories called Jokers' Cards, each of which offers a specific lesson designed to change the 'evil ways' of listeners before 'the end consumes us all.'"

Is this the musical interest of a well-adjusted, normal, happy and socially integrated person? The followers of ICP are called Juggalos.

Recently, Juggalos were classified by the FBI as a gang that "engaged in sporadic, disorganized, *individualistic crime...*". The band challenged this in court... and lost.

By this time, Keyes already possessed most of the characteristics and attitudes necessary to become both an aggressive criminal, robbing banks while armed, and, his particular pleasure, killing people. He was stashing killing kits in various locations cross the USA, which included both weapons and other paraphernalia of stealth and execution. He began funding his travels and his detailed researching of potential victims. He had an apparently normal life as a building contractor with a girlfriend and a young daughter. What was happening in his private world, the world of his mind, was, I suggest, calculating, cold, compassionless and brutal. He was morally alienated from, and contemptuous of, civilian life, which accepts rules and regulations. I think he saw himself as a highly successful and professional killer, superior to almost everyone else because he had freed himself from the mediocrity of conformity.

I would speculate that, while there may be many young men who feel alienated from conventional modern life, it is exceptional for this to be a contributing influence for their becoming a serial killer. Feelings of being outside of, or rejected by, the mainstream are usually sublimated. Keyes had an active hatred for conventional American life, it's conformity and soft comforts at the expense of risk and adventure. He was alienated to the point of pathology.

Keyes was, however, rather unusual in successfully living this double life and protective of his "normal" life partner, child and business, and I've no doubt there would have been people who knew him who were surprised that he had a vicious, dark, alter ego killer self. Most serial killers I've studied were living conspicuously dysfunctional lives. Ultimately, like many other serial killers, Keyes got sloppy and started to make mistakes. Mistakes which were eventually to lead to his capture.

Untypical mistakes

Uniquely, Keyes kidnapped and killed a young woman living in his hometown. The abduction was recorded on camera which triggered a huge search for the missing girl (who was tragically killed shortly after her abduction). Keyes left the victim's body in a shed at his home and went on a two-week cruise. This sequence of events is extraordinary given this killer's *modus operandi*, and warrants scrutiny. Given Keyes had thus far been so assiduously careful in his planning and execution, why would he, apparently on impulse, risk capture? Was it just that he got sloppy and careless? Or might he have become so smugly confident in his apparent ability to escape detection that he didn't think he'd get caught. Having uniquely killed close to home, Keyes compounded the risk by using the victim's debit card about a month after his return from his holiday. He was also recorded on an ATM camera (all this in Texas, a long way from his home in Alaska), which established the rental car he was driving, so that he was now linked to both the card and the murder. He wasn't arrested however until local police in a small Texas town stopped him for speeding—going three mph over the limit. He was originally only extradited back to Alaska on credit card fraud charges and it wasn't for another two weeks that the victim's body was discovered, and he was eventually indicted for the kidnap and murder.

This case is an excellent example of the weakness in US police jurisdictions whereby murderers need only cross state lines to lose relevant police oversight. As Keyes had victims in several states and only the last one was local, the police had no ready way to connect the cases.

Motive: "Why not?"

Understanding the motives for serial killing is, I suggest, of central interest. It is surprising and rather disappointing therefore that police seem to seldom prioritise this in questioning. In this case, however, we are told that investigators did try to determine Keyes' motives for the eight murders to which he confessed. Sadly, the best they did was to quote him as saying, "A lot of people ask why, and I would be, like, why not?" While it is entirely possible that we are being inaccurate and therefore unfair and that Keyes may have been subjected to rigorous, repeat and sustained questioning on his motives, sadly I could find no record of it.

Apparently, in the end the investigators concluded that Keyes' motivation was quite simple. "He did it because he liked it."

Well, although I never met the man, and definitely have no police experience, I am willing to presume to say Keyes *didn't* like killing. He *loved* it. And I am prepared to further speculate that his motives were power, dominance, sex and a need to create a self-image of which he could be proud, and which was consistent with his twisted and malign world view. He was testing himself as a man who was above conventional morality. I am also prepared to suggest that, if he hadn't been uncharacteristically sloppy in his last killing, Israel Keyes would have continued to kill and that many more people would have died, due in part to the unusual skill set he had which meant he was extremely organized, detailed and controlled. He wasn't caught as a result of diligent, professional and intelligent police work. He was ultimately undone by his own hubris and arrogance. That he deprived the law of due process and punishment was consistent with this arrogance and sense of superiority.

But, make no mistake. Israel Keyes was made in America.

CHAPTER FIVE
SAMUEL LITTLE: THE WORST AMERICAN SERIAL KILLER

Samuel Little: The Worst American Serial Killer

One of the sicker manifestations of the American obsession with serial killers is the competition to be the worst, or "best" depending on how sick your perspective is. And, of course, this is determined primarily by being the person who has killed the most people. The current American record holder is a man called Samuel Little, who claims to have had 93 victims and the FBI has labelled him the most prolific serial killer in USA history.[1]

Little has been imprisoned since 2014 for three murders and subsequently claimed, or boasted, of 93 victims. I haven't chosen Little for inclusion in this book because of the total number of alleged victims, but rather as an illustration of another aspect of this tragic phenomenon: the extraordinary periods which serial killers can get away with killing without being arrested, convicted and either imprisoned or in some states executed, and the extraordinary numbers killed in that timeframe. The authorities say Little confessed to carrying out these 93 killings between 1970 and 2005. Please pause, stop and consider. He travelled around the country for at least 35 years killing at least this number of women for none of which he was apprehended until finally identified by DNA. In fact, if he hadn't confessed to additional killings, we may never have known about some of them. How was this possible?

The *New York Times* published an article about Little entitled "How Did a Serial Killer Escape Notice?" and answered, rhetorically, "His victims were vulnerable and overlooked." That, at least, is undeniable.

---

1. The joint authors of one text identify Edward Wayne Edwards as the most prolific USA serial killer with 168 murders. However, like Little and also the UK's Harold Shipman, the actual total of Edwards' murders remains unverified as Edwards was only convicted of sample charges: see Anderson D C and Scott N P, 2016 in the *Selected References*.

Most of the victims were women. Most of them were black and many were poor. Most, too, were prostitutes. Some were estranged from family, isolated, and drug or alcohol dependent. I draw attention to a quote from the former police chief of Redlands California and ex-president of the National Police Foundation:

> "One of the unfortunate realities of policing is that departments that are under pressure to solve a variety of murders may pay less attention to victims from a more vulnerable population if they don't have the same organized community pressure to solve those crimes. If a killer wants to do as many murders as possible, they'll start to exploit those gaps in the social fabric and those weaknesses in law enforcement with victims that few people care about."

The explicit statement from the first part of this quote is that police "pay less attention" depending upon community pressure. So, may we assume therefore that the police response to murder or someone "going missing" is largely a product of adverse social or media pressure. Is that really how we expect investigators to behave? Secondly, is the expression "gaps in the social fabric" adequate to explain the failure to put together the pieces of someone killing nearly 100 women over those years sufficient to at least put him on a list to be questioned?

Finally, is the magnitude of care, or the number of people who have challenged the police, really an appropriate and acceptable arbiter of the strength or rigour of police investigations. And further, what are the "weaknesses in law enforcement" to which the former police chief refers? Social alienation and racial discrimination are, I assert, factors which significantly contribute to the serial killing phenomenon in the USA. In these senses at least, the individual states are conspicuously not united. Consider this hypothetical question: How many local dignitaries or famous women would Little have had to kill before the police would have mounted a successful, let alone competent, investigation? How many people would have to die before there would be justice?

The most salient factor in this serial killer's story is the questions it raises about the legal system. If the offender had been white, prosperous and professional, if the first victim had been white also, and upper-class, would there have been the same failure to inquire? There would, on balance, have been a trial and, again, on balance, the killer would have received a custodial sentence. But it could equally be argued that the person charged would have escaped being convicted by virtue of clever legal representation finding a procedural error which rendered a vital piece of evidence inadmissible. Or witness evidence may have been questioned, undermined or discredited. The list goes on and we've all read or seen enough about American jurisprudence to know these assertions are all too plausible.

So, in terms of "getting away with it", Samuel Little was extremely fortunate that he chose his victims the way he did. Is there a case to put that the American judicial system seems to have a racist cultural bias which places female black prostitutes at the bottom of the pile in terms of prioritising crime investigations based on victim profiles?

A further significant feature of Little's horrific killing life is that he was nomadic. He travelled around continental USA and killed women in at least 19 states. This meant that his crimes in one state didn't "follow him" via a sufficiently connected database to his next state. It also meant that the police in all the relevant states, cities and towns would not have co-ordinated their enquiries. The killings would not easily have been linked.

Little's story

Samuel Little is black. He was born Samuel McDowell in Reynolds, Georgia, in 1940. He claims his mother was a prostitute and that she abandoned him. One source suggests she gave birth to him while she was in jail. He was raised by his grandmother. From an early age, Little behaved poorly, was aggressive and academically poor. Available records of his early life are limited and fragmentary, but he clearly developed anti-authority, criminal patterns as early as his fifteenth year, when he was convicted of breaking and entering.

He also clearly was roaming freely across the USA from a relatively young age, where whilst still in his twenties he managed to be arrested in eight different states for rape, armed robbery, aggravated assault, solicitation, fraud, shoplifting and driving under the influence. During one of his many prison stints, he learned boxing, later describing himself as a prize fighter. By his thirty-fifth year, Little had been arrested 26 times in eleven states. It would seem that, by this stage, he had already killed more than once, but we know little of these crimes beyond his own accounts given when he was eventually imprisoned over 30 years later. What is recorded next may leave you speechless.

In 1982, aged 42, Little was arrested in Mississippi and charged with the murder of a 22-year-old woman. We have no details, but it is reported that "A grand jury declined to indict Little for the murder…". While still under investigation for this offence, Little was transferred to Florida for trial for another murder. This too was of a young woman whose body had been found during the same year. Despite substantive witness evidence against him, and apparently due to "mistrust of witness testimonies", Little was acquitted. So, in the same year, he managed to either escape being indicted or was acquitted of two separate murders. Am I alone in wondering whether the jury in the second trial were aware that he had only recently been freed from another murder charge? Probably not as that would been seen as prejudicial unless some pattern were evidenced and that pattern was seemingly not picked-up on by prosecutors. Is there a reason to ask questions concerning the circumstances which occasioned sufficient mistrust in the evidence to release him? The question of both judicial competence and institutional racial and class prejudice is indelible and compelling. The result is that Little was free to kill again.

Having moved states yet again, Little was next arrested two years later and charged with kidnapping, beating and attempting to strangle another 22-year-old woman, but one who survived. Extraordinarily, he must have been released (not remanded in custody for these serious, violent and life threatening charges), because he was found one month later by police "in the back seat of his car with an unconscious woman, also beaten and strangled in the same location as the attempted murder" a month earlier. He was convicted of both crimes and served two-and-a-half years in prison. That is less prison time than is normally served for significantly less serious crimes. Little had kidnapped, beaten, strangled and almost killed two women and served just 30 months for these horrific crimes.

The recommended sentence for attempted murder in the first degree in the USA is capital punishment (where available) or life imprisonment. Otherwise, it is five to nine years. Arguably, if Little had been convicted of the lesser charge on two counts, he should have expected a sentence of between ten and 18 years! I wonder what sentence he'd have received if the victims had been white, middle-class, professional women. Whatever, Little was free to kill again. And he did. Upon his release in February 1987, he moved immediately to Los Angeles and committed more than ten additional murders. It is impossible to escape the impression that there had to have been opportunities during these years for Little to be apprehended and I can think of no more resounding indictment of the American criminal justice system, including both the courts and the police, than this case.

Fifteen years later, in 2012, Little was arrested on the basis of DNA-evidence which linked him to three murders, committed between 1987 and 1989.

From Samuel Little's own mouth

When he was interviewed for a TV programme, Little said:

"I loved all the women."

And he laughed when saying it. His first killing was, he says, in 1970. He recalled it thus:

"Bless her heart."

"When they die, they're all your favourites. They all belong to you."

"God, I got so crazy. I wanted more."

He said he killed them all in the same way: strangulation.

"Put my hands around the throat. She evidently wanted this to happen."

He said that from a very young age, four or five in school, he looked at his teacher rubbing her throat and he was sexually aroused. When asked why it took him until he was 30 to start killing, he said he had just been imagining it for years. Crucially, he acknowledged that he had chosen prostitutes for all his victims, almost all black women, and that:

"There weren't no women nurses and teachers. That's the reason I didn't get busted a long time ago."

"See, a lot of these women they have a death wish."

He said they were his friends. The Mail Online website reported that Little "… put his huge, boxer's hands to lethal use, knocking the women senseless with a single punch before throttling the life out of them." When finally induced to sketch his victims "portraits", he noted on one: "Sam killed me but I love him." Recalling another murder, Little said, while almost laughing: "You know that she's fighting for her life and I'm fighting for my pleasure." Asked what drove him to kill, he said, "God put me on Earth to do what I did. He made me."

Only one of his victims ever got away. In 1976, she managed to escape while stripped to the waist and with her hands tied behind her back with electrical cord. She had been picked-up, choked and raped. Little received three months' imprisonment. I suspect if she hadn't been a black prostitute Little's sentence would have been over ten times longer.

The above quotes are illuminating and tell us a great deal about this serial killer's psychology. They are classic examples of the defence mechanisms of minimalisation and denial. From asserting he was sexually excited by his teacher's neck when aged four or five, all the way through to blaming God, Samuel Little is full of pathetic excuses, lies, denials and deceptions. He never uses the words kidnap, coerce, rape or kill. He portrays his deeds as intuitive acts of affirmation. He didn't rape, they had consensual sex. He didn't murder because they wanted to die. He didn't hate his victims. He loved them.

Little has no conscience in the conventional moral sense. That would require him to be able to distinguish between right and wrong and to apply this distinction to his behaviour, his life. In addition to being an historically evil serial killer, Little was a lifelong criminal who spent his entire adult life taking and abusing. He was a lazy sociopath. His statements are from the mind of a man who feels a casual indifference to killing. In fact, he has rationalised and excused killing these women by the repulsive assertion that they had a wish for him to kill them. Equally, his claim to have loved them is both a lie and another fabrication of denial, in which he asserts the act of killing was an act of love.

For Little, there is no guilt because he has done nothing wrong. Raping and killing, or even consensual sex with a prostitute, was also about power and ego enhancement. He did nothing with his life. He was a failure. Without the killings, he was invisible and insignificant. He enjoyed killing and spent his life doing it and getting away with it because he lived in a country seemingly indifferent to the lives of black prostitutes.

I reviewed much of the records concerning the police and court response to Little's many years of serial killing. The entire record is focused on Little and on describing what he did, especially the remarkable display of colour drawings he made to help the police identify the victims and clear-up open records across America. There is nothing about how it all happened. About how he was able to get away with it. Or what made him what he is.

No conventional conscience

Samuel Little has no conventional social conscience. He became a criminal early in his life because, presumably, he had never been taught right from wrong. It is entirely speculative, but he may have learned early on to harbour hostile, negative feelings towards prostitutes due to his mother having been both a poor mother who abandoned him to his grandmother and having been a prostitute herself. The overwhelming majority of his victims were black prostitutes and it is obvious that his primary motives were sex and dominance. There is not one spark of compassion or any feelings of regret for his monstrous deeds. In a wider, more significant sense, Samuel Little personifies much that has gone wrong with contemporary, rootless, amoral America. He:

- was born to a black prostitute who deserted him
- lived a life of casual, transient crime interspersed with equally casual killing
- demonstrates class and race-based prejudice in America which counts black female prostitutes as disposable. As stated, if Little had killed white middle-class professional women, he would not have been free to travel the continent killing for 35 years; and

- his case shows that the courts and police had several opportunities to arrest, try and convict him and failed to do so.

When he was initially caught, his punishment was inexplicably light, enabling him to soon kill again rather than being imprisoned. When he did eventually confess to over 90 murders, although he had only been convicted of three, it was Little who disclosed the rest, and only then due to the cautious befriending, non-judgemental approach of one interrogator. There was no recognition that Samuel Little's life of serial killing was in any way a result of anything other than his own mental instability or proclivities. No reference to the crucial life influences, as that would place a degree of responsibility on the American lifestyle he chose to live. He described what he did as an act of friendship done with compliant, even willing, women. I could find no record of this sickening distortion being challenged.

All the American media attention on Little has focused on the number of his victims and the drawings and paintings he made of them; on how impressively detailed his drawings and accounts of the killings are after so many years. While it is entirely understandable that the police across the country would want to clear-up outstanding murders, most of which had been wrongly recorded as "other than murder", is it a form of institutional denial that he is a product of place, and that, if he hadn't been born and raised in the USA, he very probably would never have killed?

Psychology of Samuel Little

The psychology of this serial killer is characterised by a mind devoid of any sense of social conscience and moral responsibility. He is delusional and dissociated from his killings and barely mentions that they were sexual acts of casual, indifferent cruelty. In describing all those dead women as his babies, and saying that they "wanted it", he both condescends as if he were paternal and denies the seriousness of his crimes. He, like so many serial killers, is in reality an insignificant loser whose only claim to fame is his dreadful killings, so it is no surprise that he has revelled in the notoriety. He would have imagined that his serial killing was a form of potent masculine achievement, a lifetime of manly dominance over inconsequential women who loved him and wanted him to kill them. Sickening, but possible.

It is an indictment of both the man and those aspects of the country which allowed it to happen. I can't think of another country which could have produced Samuel Little. He is an all-American serial killer.

CHAPTER SIX
ROBERT BLACK: THE DEPRAVED

Robert Black: The Depraved

Robert Black was born in Scotland in 1947. He became an horrific paedophilic serial killer of little girls. In 1994 he was convicted of the kidnap, rape and murder of three victims; having been arrested with a further, six-year-old girl, hooded, gagged and bound in his delivery van. He had sexually-abused her shortly before being caught. He was later, in 2011, convicted of the murder of a fourth victim. He had earlier convictions in Scotland as a juvenile for kidnap and sexual assault. There were many other unsolved similar crimes for which Black (who died in prison in 2016 aged 68) remains the prime suspect.

If you shone a light into the darkest place, it would be reflected in Black's dead, depraved, evil eyes. At one point, as I was reading the details of his crimes, I became so distressed I began to cry and had to stop and walk away. I am reluctant to record here any details of his crimes and will only mention the minimum possible to explain including him. They are closely catalogued in other books, such as the work of Ray Wyre, Tim Tate and Charmaine Richardson noted in the *Selected References*.

Childhood

Black was an illegitimate child of an unknown father and a mother who wanted to put him up for adoption, then abandoned him in order to emigrate and never saw him again. There was evidence of physical abuse from foster parents. At the age of five, Black and a little girl compared genitalia, triggering a belief in Black, allegedly, that he should have been born female. Whatever, he developed a deep fascination in his genitals and the genitalia of female children (all this according to Black's own statements). He also said that, from the age of eight, he inserted objects into his anus. He continued this pattern throughout his offending. He had a morbid fascination with sex and his body from a relatively early age.

According to sources reporting his early years, Black was an aggressive and unpopular child, given to tantrums and vandalism. A target for bullies, he soon became one himself. His nickname in school was apparently 'Smelly Bobby Tulip', after he had adopted the surname of his rather old foster parents.

At primary school, Black (then called Tulip) became an aggressive bully, including physical beatings of younger, weaker children, even of a disabled boy with an artificial leg. This pattern would have reinforced in him that he had the ability to be dominant and abusive to younger children and get away with it. This is an extremely strong learning experience which was clearly stored away for future, lethal, use. His childhood fascination with genitalia and rectal self-penetration were manifestations of his sexual immaturity and ambivalence, but also of an increasingly morbid interest in criminal predation.

When his first foster parents died (the foster father may have physically abused him), he was placed with a second foster family. It was soon after this that he committed his first known sexual assault, by dragging a young girl into a public lavatory and fondling her. As a result of this, the second foster parents had him removed from their home. Despite his existing history of inserting objects into his anus, and of having sexually assaulted a younger girl, he was placed next in a mixed sex children's home. This unfortunate and arguably ill-judged placement resulted in Black exposing himself repeatedly to young girls who were resident in the home and, not surprisingly, he found himself "kicked out" again. This time, he was placed in what was described as a "high-discipline all male establishment". Here, instead of Black abusing others, apparently, he was the victim of sexual assaults by a male staff member for a period of three years. These assaults included forced fellatio.

The psychological effects of being victim rather than abuser would have taught Black (or reinforced pre-existing learned behaviour) that it is far better to be the abuser than the victim, and that sex is something to be forced rather than asked for or as a natural progression in a loving or passionate relationship. Black never experienced the latter so would not have known what it was like or that it was possible. He knew from experience that *all* those who had been responsible for him had, in one way or another, failed him, and that many of the most powerful ones had physically or sexually abused him. He also knew from experience that he could sexually molest and rape little girls and get away with it. He had learned what to do to satisfy his perverted sexual needs. It cannot be overemphasised how critical this history of childhood abuse and rejection would have been concerning Black's emotional development. He was completely and irreversibly damaged and depraved, especially in how he fantasised about and imagined sexual gratification.

By this stage in his life, Robert Black would I suggest have been beyond saving. Barely a teenager, I believe he was already a fully committed sexual deviant who would target young girls for the rest of his life. His primary sexual orientation was one of arrested development and although he made attempts in later life to have adult relationships they failed. The act of inserting objects into his anus was confirmed in photographs police found on him after his arrest in 1990, including of him having inserted a wine bottle, a telephone handset and a table leg. This aberration seems to be homosexual self-abuse but, while it may have been, Black never manifested any known sexual attraction towards men or young boys. He is recorded as having said he would have preferred to have been a girl, but he was obviously a "sexual mutant".

When he was 16, Black left the care of the local authority and got a job as a delivery boy. This was clearly an opportunistic employment, as Black reported having sexually fondled 30-40 children in various houses to which he was delivering without ever being caught or reported. This sequence of escalating paedophilic behaviour simply put in place the conditions and learning for Black's graduation to abduction, abuse and killing. I could find no record of care agencies, social services or the police having intervened effectively in the Black case, even when there was clear and repeated evidence that he was becoming a serious risk to young girls.

An "isolated incident"

What happened next was perhaps then not only not surprising but inevitable. It was in 1963 that Black was convicted of taking a seven-year-old girl into a deserted air-raid shelter, holding her by the throat until she passed out, and masturbating over her. He was arrested and interviewed by a psychiatrist, who suggested "the incident was an isolated one, and that Black was not in need of treatment." As a result, Black was "admonished" for the offence. This for a violent sexual assault where the victim could have died! And where the victim, a seven-year-old girl, would have been severely traumatised.

If this is in fact the case, one wonders whether that psychiatrist subsequently read of Black's serial killing career with untold numbers of victims of abuse and reflected both on his professional judgement and conscience. What would it have taken for the psychiatrist to have considered him to be a risk! This result must have strongly reinforced Black's deviant and dangerous behaviour, as it constituted positive reinforcement, i.e. when he did something which he enjoyed and was not punished for it, that increased the probability he would do it again. His record from then on is full of sexual molestation of female children and of not being punished, or of "charges dropped".

Escalating offending and missed opportunities

He was constantly abusing girls throughout his life and getting away with it. When he did eventually start killing his victims (the first known case of this was in 1981, but there may well have been precedents as early as 1969), I suspect it was partly a need to safeguard against being caught as well as the next perverse stage in his descent into depravity. His was a classic learning pattern of escalating offending over many years with little or no punishment. It was of increasing brutality and he had a need to feed his obsession by increasingly grotesque acts. He drove throughout the United Kingdom, and in Europe, as a delivery driver, affording him a plausible excuse and countless opportunities for anonymous kidnapping. He was isolated and friendless, with no wife or family.

Black's life was a succession of rejections. In his late teens, he moved to a quiet part of Northern England where he lodged with an elderly couple. He began dating a young woman he'd met at a youth club and she became his only known girlfriend. After the relationship had developed and deepened over months, Black asked her to marry him, and was devastated when she rejected him and ended the relationship, in part apparently due to his unusual sexual demands. A short time later, in 1966, Black's landlord discovered he had molested their nine-year-old granddaughter repeatedly when she had visited them. Although they kicked him out, crucially they failed to notify the police, wanting to spare the victim further trauma. This failure to prosecute Black was to be repeated time-and-again and is, with the benefit of reflection, an unmitigated tragedy.

Still only a teenager and living in Scotland, Black found new lodgings. Aged 19, his latest landlords informed police that he had repeatedly molested their daughter. He pleaded guilty to three counts of indecent assault and was given a borstal sentence of one year. He was sent to, Polmont, which was officially meant to "specialise in training and rehabilitation". It clearly didn't work with Black and, as he refused throughout his life to speak of his time there, we can only speculate that, yet again, there was abuse. This was to be the last stage of his life in Scotland.

Black moved south to London in September 1968. He found a job as a lifeguard at a swimming pool where within weeks he was fired for fondling a young girl. Yet again, no charges were brought. He would have learned or had reinforced at this stage that he could offend with only a very low risk of punishment. This is classic learning and would have confirmed to Black that the risk was worth taking.

He soon gravitated towards pornography, specialising in graphic child sexual abuse. This would, of course, have fuelled his already uncontrolled fantasies and drives to abuse young girls. A not insignificant interest in photography allowed him to secretly photograph or film young girls at swimming pools and add these to his growing store of pornography which he kept in suitcases at his lodgings.

In 1972, Black met and moved in with a Scottish couple and lived in their attic until his arrest 18 years later. This couple reported knowing Black used pornography but claimed to have no idea it was paedophilic.

Black now moved, deliberately, to significantly enhance his ability to live a successful life as a full-time lethal paedophile. In 1976, aged 29, he got a job as a despatch driver. The stage was set for the worst to unfold. He was at this stage in his life a completely compromised human being, given over irretrievably to finding, abusing and killing young girls, even children. Although it wasn't until 1981 that he was later proved to have committed an abduction and murder, I have little doubt in my own professional assessment that there were earlier victims. Black soon developed a comprehensive knowledge of the UK road system enabling him to find children and abduct them and then take their bodies long distances from the sites of the abductions before disposing of their bodies.

Black's psychology

There has been a great deal printed about this "appalling life form", Robert Black. Most of it focuses on the forensic aspects: details of his crimes, enormous and lengthy attempts by co-ordinated police forces to find him, and the trials which eventually found him guilty. I could find little about the psychology of this serial killer and his hideous thinking. He was attacked once in prison and received relatively minor injuries. Because of his victims, I have the most disturbing feelings of wanting to visit a more severe punishment upon him than that which the state eventually provided, life imprisonment with a whole life tariff; thinking that I might have welcomed capital punishment for him; and that even that would have been completely inadequate. That he was the sort of person such punishment was meant for; and that it is a pity it wasn't available for him. No doubt others will disagree.

As for his psychology, he was a product of abuse from a very early age. His childhood of prematurely deviant sexual interests was triggered by his own developing sexual ambiguity and by repeated sexually perverse acts to which he was subjected by those responsible for "parenting" him; then those in institutions responsible for his safety and care; finally his own deviant drives to force sex upon female children. His only experience of an adult relationship with a woman failed and he was rejected. He turned back to the arrested sexual development where he targeted female children who could not reject him and were only objects for his gratification.

He was able to access deviant material to feed his perversions, to find jobs which facilitated them, and by travelling extensively around both the UK and Europe, leave a relatively untraceable trail of abduction, abuse, rape and murder. He enjoyed all these experiences, which he skilfully hid for years. He learned over these years how to be successful in his malignant desires, both in his methods and in his avoidance of arrest. I have no doubt he would, if not stopped, have continued his life of paedophilic horror until he died. It is a tragedy that it took so long to catch him, despite one of the longest, most complex, detailed, and expensive UK police operations ever.

Because of the relatively early onset of his deviant sexual behaviour, it could be argued that Black was "born that way" and that his lack of nurturing simply served to feed those tendencies — and it may be difficult to argue against this. But, if Robert Black had had loving, supportive and protective parents, lived in a friendly and law-abiding neighbourhood, gone to schools where there were robust rules and supportive staff, not been sexually abused repeatedly throughout his childhood and adolescence, been proportionately punished when he first experimented with sexual deviance and abusing girls, and been seen by more competent psychiatrists, I presume to suggest he would never have become the monster that he did.

Black's sexual orientation is confused, but there are those who would argue that he was simply a conflicted transsexual who, in more liberal, contemporary times would have been able to access services to aid him in his "journey" towards realising his true self. I don't personally subscribe to that view. There are by my own assessment just two genders and everything we think relevant to sex is a product of which biological sex we are born with, and our life experiences thereafter. Any elaboration on these views is not relevant to this book (other than perhaps to note that official gender recognition has of recent times been moving in the opposite direction). Suffice it to say, I believe Black was a product of the experiences he had as a child and young adult. Abusive experiences significantly increase the risk of becoming an abusive adult. Severely abusive experiences can lead to a severely abusive (murderous) adult. Not always. Simply that this is significantly more likely.

Rationalisation

Once Robert Black abducted a young girl, sexually abused her and killed her, the consequences were critical as to whether he would do so again. He would have been sexually gratified. He would have enjoyed the power and control and would have seen what he did as successful. He was not caught so he was not punished. His crimes were premeditated; he would think through what he would do and ensure he did the abducting in a safe, secret place. He would have had no feelings of guilt, remorse or contrition, because he did not see his victims as children. He would have rationalised to himself that killing them after what he'd done to them was almost merciful, as the trauma they would have felt would have been worse had they lived. Dead, they felt nothing. He would have thought about the long investigation and been elated at his success in evading it.

I suspect there were many times when Black was enjoying a pint at his local or chatting to his workmates, and the subject of the police hunt came up, when he would have wanted to show off his knowledge of the crimes. He would have been proud of his ongoing success at eluding capture and seen himself as successful and, potentially, famous. There would never have been a moment when he thought of the terrible things he'd done and of the children, their families and the agonies he caused.

Robert Black had no conscience. He had no compassion. He was a "dead man walking". I read one book in about him (more accurately a book written to profit from the prurient public appetite for horror) descriptive of the killings and the police investigations and that tells us little about the psychology of this dreadful serial killer. I hope this chapter has gone some way towards rectifying that. The only solace is that it is exceptionally rare to create this magnitude of monster. But the horror is that it is possible.

CHAPTER SEVEN
MICHAEL BRUCE ROSS: FEELING MORE REAL

Michael Bruce Ross: Feeling More Real

Ross was a sexually inadequate American serial killer who took the lives of eight girls and women aged between 14 and 25. Interviewed in prison, he said that he strangled them because it gave him more of a connection; he felt more real. He would kidnap, gag, rape and strangle. He was recorded to have confessed that:

> "They were dead as soon as I saw them. The smallest: it was so close to the ideal, it was like a fantasy. That one bothered me the most. She was so small and co-operative."

These sickening thoughts contained in a direct quote tell us a great deal about the psychology of this otherwise completely innocuous man. His is a story of someone who was a cowardly failure in his relationships with women and who resorted to stalking, raping and murdering to satisfy his sexual inadequacy.

Formative years and events

Ross' childhood and formative years followed a predictable pattern. His home life was extremely dysfunctional, difficult and unpredictable. His mother was psychologically unstable. She is recorded to have beaten all four of her children, with Michael receiving the worst of this punishment. His parents were unhappily married. Ross was a bright student and did well at school. Possibly as a safe alternative to the chaos at home, he would have enjoyed his academic opportunities. Rare for serial killers, he went on from high school to a good university, Cornell, in New

York state. He studied agriculture, mainly as his family had had a farm in his home state of Connecticut.

Rather, it is the adolescent and young adult Ross to whom we must address our scrutiny. When he said the victims were dead as soon as he saw them, it is both an attempt to minimise his personal culpability by implying he had little or no control over his urges, and also that he was targeting a certain type of young woman. This is premeditation. If he was aware of his extreme reactions to certain women, did he seek help? Did he try and control his thoughts? When did normal relationships no longer supply an alternative? When he refers to regrets about a particularly small and compliant victim, it is a grotesque expression of false compassion. He was signalling that she was his ideal victim except that she was too decent and that he would have preferred a struggle which would have been more satisfying to his need for dominance over women. His victims were small and young, presenting little or no risk of physical resistance. Ross felt that he was a failure with women, and he was right. He was taking his revenge on them so long as he could find young, vulnerable and attractive targets.

The long, slow process of desensitisation towards attacking women, and the disinhibition of that first, critical attack being successful, were key events in the making of this pathetic, inadequate but calculating and deviant serial killer. He learned to objectify women. He learned to target young women and strike in safe, isolated places. He learned from rejection that he could not achieve sufficiently stable long-term relationships to gratify his sex drive. He learned that he could abduct and rape and get away with it. He learned that, if he was to continue pleasuring himself by abducting and raping, he would have to kill. He learned that, when he abducted, raped and killed women, he enjoyed it even more.

In a pathetic attempt to explain his murders, Ross said, "It seems to be both biological ... something wrong with my head, and the way I was raised." He spoke of when he was young, when he would fantasise that he would "kidnap women and take them to my place of safety and they would fall in love with me ... James Bond sort of thing." While obviously a sexually frustrated, deluded fantasist, Ross is expressing an almost childlike naïvety and rather sad fantasy world, one which he would have nurtured and developed into a plan.

I could find no record of any girlfriends during high school, which would have been a time where his sexual drive would have been very high, so I would imagine a great deal of frustration, fantasy and masturbation. Ross confessed that, when he went to college, aged 18, these fantasies degenerated into thoughts and images including rape, then rape with violence. He then said he started following women and getting aroused, then fantasising. These fantasies would become rehearsals until the anger and frustration grew to the point of explosion. This is a recognised pattern of serial killing. First comes the creation of the abused wanting to be the abuser. Then, over time and if sexually inadequate and frustrated, the resentment and anger.

When these thoughts become so strong, they are invasive, we see them as obsessive. When a sexual obsession is linked to compulsive masturbation and the use of pornography as a substitute for actual intercourse, we see the first stage of compulsion, which is the behaviour fathered by the thought. The next stage could be something as relatively mild as voyeurism or becoming a "peeping-tom".

Escalation and returning drives

The escalation proceeds to sexual assault and rape. But sex is a biological drive which, as soon as it is satiated, returns; and, with it, the impetus. The risk of capture is obvious, so the rapist becomes a killer as an act of self-preservation. There is often an additional function in killing as an act of retaliation towards women for rejection, and of bitterness because the perpetrator will know at some level of thought that he is an abject failure. We might even view masturbation in these cases as a form of arrested development, where the man's maturation into a successful heterosexual being is stunted and deformed.

Not long after going to university, Ross had his first serious relationship with another student. Tragically, she became pregnant and aborted the child, which triggered a decline in the relationship, one in which Ross had considered proposing marriage, until it deteriorated through increasingly severe arguments until she left him. This rejection may have been a staging post towards his descent into depravity, feeding his growing but suppressed, feelings of interpersonal inadequacy.

Progression to serial offending

As a senior at Cornell, and while he was still involved in a second doomed relationship, Ross committed his first rape, saying later in interview after his arrest (see further below) that his violent sexual fantasies had by then "consumed" him. The pattern, once the rape was successful and he was not caught, was now fixed. Over the next three years until his arrest, Ross went on to abduct, rape and kill eight women. There was a striking absence of any emotion or contrition towards the victims when he was interviewed. They meant nothing to him. They were anonymous, sexual objects.

Ross became dangerously disinhibited during this crucial period, such that he would not have stopped and, I suspect, his assaults would have degenerated further with greater deviant violence and sex being practised on his victims. He was clearly obsessive-compulsive and remained a total risk of killing again. He acknowledged this risk, saying "My biggest thrill sexually is actually killing young girls." Not the raping; the killing. And not women — girls.

When imprisoned, he was recorded as saying, "I would re-live my killings multiple times a day. I would masturbate several times a day to these images to the point of having sores on myself." No doubt this was a pattern before capture as well. Ross asked to be castrated while in custody due to sexual frustration at not being able to rape and kill to gratify his sexual urges. My feeling is that he wouldn't have gone through with it, and was simply using this as part of his efforts to show the magnitude of his false contrition.

Sadly, we can record that twice during the three year long killing spree, Ross was arrested for sexual assaults and let off with light punishment to continue raping and killing. Why? After arrest, it was discovered he had been on probation in Illinois in 1981 for threatening a woman and jailed for four months in 1982 in Ohio after assaulting a woman in her house. Neither of these convictions would, it seems, have been available in Connecticut to the police during the crucial period of his killing spree. It would seem the gaps between police forces, where criminals' records don't routinely follow offenders from state to state, were to have lethal consequences.

This serial killer's thinking and psychology

Psychiatrists said that Ross was sexually abused by an uncle and in turn molested girls. I'm not sure I understand the reasoning as to how that logically follows. It is a specious argument. Ross maintained he couldn't control himself, but he selected his victims, stalked those who fitted his profile and in settings which were safe, and he engaged in detailed and successful hiding of the bodies and avoiding capture for three years.

It is typical of killers that they rationalise their behaviour in order to minimise culpability and displace blame onto others, or onto "uncontrollable urges". There are in my view no uncontrollable urges, only weak people. There are no sexual addicts. Only people who fail to control their biological drives and who have inadequately developed social and moral precepts. People who take personal responsibility are an endangered species.

Ross strikes me a as a highly manipulative, intelligent, callous, totally self-obsessed sexual sadist (I have said elsewhere that this is no excuse). He was obviously inadequate in his sex life. How he became a serial sexual killer is not really that complicated. I think his childhood was particularly significant in terms of causation, especially from the experience of abusive, over-punitive parents. It is clear from both the accounts of those who knew the family and from Ross himself that his mother was an extremely abusive, domineering and unstable influence. Ross' attitude to the two young women he eventually had serious relationships with were significantly influenced and tainted by his subconscious associations with them when they were assertive or confrontational, just as his mother had been.

I believe he hated his mother. There are many stories of her forcing him by the strength of her personality to do things which he hated, like putting the family dog to sleep when it wasn't necessary. It was probably also significant that Ross had no sexual experience as a teenager in high school. He left home a virgin. He had already, not surprisingly, resorted to almost obsessional masturbation while still at home, which may have been one of the reasons why his mother is reported to have dragged Ross' mattress out of the house when he left home for university, doused it in petrol and set fire to it. Ross left home an extremely sexually repressed young man who was probably already harbouring repressed hatred of women while being desperate to experience sex.

Free from his oppressive, controlling mother, Ross went to Cornell University to study Agriculture, the obvious choice given his family's farming lifestyle. There, he quickly set out to find and have sex with any young woman who would comply. He had two significant relationships. The first ended not long after the woman had become pregnant and had an abortion. Ross behaved predictably badly towards her, offering no support as he was totally unprepared for adult responsibilities and had never experienced a reciprocal loving mature relationship. Being with a woman was how he could have sex. That was essentially the extent of his interpersonal skills at that stage. I speculate that this may also have been the period when he began to have invasive dark thoughts and fantasies of forcing himself on women. The only serious relationship he'd had to date ended with the woman taking charge of it and making the important decisions. It may have triggered suppressed resentment and anger in him; an unacknowledged and nagging thought that perhaps he was inadequate as a man.

Ross' second serious relationship began within days of the end of his first, showing perhaps how superficial and sexually obsessed he was. His own description of how it ended is telling: "That's what I was afraid of. I didn't want her to know how much power she had over me, how much I cared. I was madly in love… or I thought I was. Now I think it was infatuation, sexual attraction, and nothing else." He couldn't cope with assertive, confident women. He acquiesced to his mother and now he was giving into women he thought of marrying. This second woman reported that they fought as their relationship began to fail. Martha Elliott in her book *The Man in the Monster*, says that because he felt another woman had power over him, as Ross said, he "…fantasised forcing my penis in her mouth, making her relive her demons". She had confided in Ross that she had been sexually assaulted in this manner previously by a stranger. This is a terribly significant confession by him. He now had several of the key elements in his psychology that would lead to the first lethal assault.

Excuses, distortion and false compassion

Michael Ross was given six death sentences. The Connecticut Supreme Court overturned them all and enabled him to spend the next 18 years living in relative comfort and no little notoriety, "finding God" and enabling him to become, allegedly, born again. He spent 18 years in prison, enjoying his notoriety and correspondence with various media and legal entities, an all too familiar pattern with American serial killers. Although he apparently attempted suicide in prison more than once, my experience of those who do so is that the attempts are often not genuine, and Ross doesn't deserve any speculation as to motives in his case. What is exceptional however is that, extremely rare for serial killers, we have an extensive and illuminating record of him and how he became the extreme deviant he was.

I discovered Martha Elliott's book (above) during my research. By then, editor and publisher of the *Connecticut Law Tribune*, she recounts her experience of a ten-year relationship with Ross. I was originally critical and dismissive as I began reading it. It was patently from the perspective of an advocate against capital punishment and the writer seemed to be arguing from a subjective and pre-determined bias. But I am grateful to have found it. It is a wonderful illustration of so many aspects of serial killing which deserve to be explored. The author is honest and reasoned, she argues the case against capital punishment, and most importantly, she provides what I think is one of the best explanations of the internal reality of a serial killer extant. And she achieved that by earning the trust of Michael Ross enough for him to candidly, and chillingly, describe his reality leading up to and during the act of killing. While I praise these achievements, I disagree with several important positions she takes towards Ross. Early in the book, she says that he was:

> "...a brutal rapist and killer, but I also met another side of him—a caring, thoughtful person who exhibited true remorse, perhaps in part because of the Christian faith he had developed..."

This assertion put me in mind of the report that Hitler was kind to children. Presumably, the fact that Ross had escaped the death penalty in Connecticut gave him the opportunity he deprived his many victims of. When the scales of justice are set against us, we are measured by both our achievements and our transgressions. When he raped and killed eight women, my view is that he forfeited his right to any sympathy whatsoever, and whatever subsequent apparent repentance and faith he expresses is both irrelevant and contemptible.

In the book Elliott says, "I deplore violence, and I do not wish to mitigate what Michael Ross did before his 1984 arrest." She then spends much of her book doing just that, by arguing he was suffering from "sexual sadism" and that as a result his culpability was diminished and that he couldn't help himself. The psychiatrists for the defence had argued that the diagnostic description was sexual sadism and that this was a mental illness. Further, when questioned as to Ross' particular affliction, Dr Berlin said it was "recurrent erotic urges and fantasies that drive [the sadism]". He explained these urges were "driven by a powerful biological drive." Well, yes, they would be, wouldn't they?

When Elliott asked the doctor how a person could become a sexual sadist, he replied, "The question is really how do any of us develop the sexual desires that we have." And, "Those feelings well up inside because of our biology, because of chromosomes and hormones and areas of the brain that are clearly relevant to sexuality." I don't know about you, but as an explanation for this particular serial killer's behaviour, that falls well short of sufficient. A cognitive behavioural approach on the other hand would look to the critical formative experiences in Ross' life, such as his deeply traumatic childhood under a tyrannical, unstable, bitter and rejecting mother, and his failures to establish and maintain normal, healthy sexual relationships with adult women.

When he was in prison, and they had initiated a relationship and she had published an article on Ross, Elliott says she had no intention of contacting him again, but that he kept calling, "desperate for human contact". She relented because "it seemed cruel to stop taking his calls. I decided that continuing to talk with him was a small effort compared with what it meant to this lonely, haunted man." Firstly, Ross would have had all the human contact he could handle in prison. Secondly, I presume to suggest Elliott's compassion might have been put to better effect comforting the families and friends of Ross' victims, who would no doubt have suffered rather more than the serial killer who ruined their lives.

Elliott records that the state of Connecticut's expert psychiatrist, Dr Robert Miller, changed his view to agree that Ross was suffering from mental-illness because: "Dr Miller wrote that he believed Michael's mental illness played a significant role in the murders...". He continued: "If it had been only one or two (murders) I could have held up, but the repetitive nature of the acts as well as past history of assaultive behaviour make my (our) position untenable." If we applied that logic as a general principle, we would have to conclude that all serial killers were mentally-ill and therefore cannot be incarcerated for life (or executed) by virtue of their having killed more than two people. This slightly absurd tautological generalisation has, fortunately, not been followed.

One diagnosis to which I would assent was from a psychiatrist named John Cegalis, who described Ross as "immature, egocentric, manipulative, driven to a kind of sexual satisfaction that fuses aggression and sexuality together in a highly abnormal way."

Perhaps the most important passage in the book, and one which is enough justification alone for all those years of contact, is one where Elliott invites Ross to "describe his violent sexual fantasies". She reports that this was only successful after several years of contact. What he produced is, in my professional opinion, one of the most important records of serial killer revelations there is. It is terribly difficult to read, but I feel some of it must be reproduced here. He recorded six pages of this hor-rific monologue of which the following are illustrative;

> "I see her. She is still 100 yards away, walking along the road …I am getting closer to her. She's small, a dirty-blond, young. She…has no idea of the danger she is in. I feel a sense of contempt because of this…She thinks that she is strong, independent and can handle herself. She is so foolish…My contempt for her ignorance continues to grow…"

> "'You stupid, arrogant bitch' I'm thinking. With every step my anger and contempt for her grows. She is so stupid to not see the danger…I want to hurt her now. I want to show her that I'm not some impotent fool to be so lightly dismissed."

> "She is nothing but a foolish, petty, ignorant bitch. She must be taught to see the truth…I want her to see and experience my control…She's going to die. I know this, but I want her to understand why first."

Ross goes on to describe in execrable detail his fantasy of cruel, aggres-sive rape and murder and the accompanying orgasm and sense of power. This was a record of something which he repeated time-and-again in prison to feed his masturbation, which was as obsessive as it had been when he was free. If you want to know what goes through the mind of a sadistic serial killer, you will find no clearer account. Straight from the monster's mind and mouth.

Elliott's book is exceptional for several important reasons. Her success in sustaining a relationship of trust with Ross over a period sufficient for him to confide in her makes it the only book written on a serial killer I know of which actually has the killer explaining absolutely clearly his own psychological chemistry, his motives, drives and the entire pattern of gradual, successive escalations towards the sex and killing. For this, she deserves great credit. Again to illustrate, she lays out so much of what we need in order to understand him:

"Rape became incorporated into my fantasies after I met Betsy [in] my junior year."

"On occasion, I used sex to hurt her. In my fantasies, sex became a way to degrade a woman."

This mental process fed his disorder of personality. Elliott explains:

"As Michael's anger and frustration … increased, the fantasies and the urges became a constant torment. Now the fantasies were not only of degradation and rape, but also of murder."

This is textbook explanation. Ross was fantasising, and fantasising is a form of rehearsal, especially if the will is weak and the drive is strengthening. Ross was not able to reconcile his inadequate attempts for a successful relationship with a woman. He was instead merging his fixated hatred of his mother and her dominance which had made his life so miserable and against which he had failed to assert himself, with his current failing relationship with Betsy. He was becoming an increasing danger of acting-out these thoughts and urges on innocent strangers. He could not inflict them on someone he knew, and he was extremely aware of the risks of detection and humiliation if he gave vent to them.

Ross then described the gradual, staged process from fantasy to reality: "Stalking was the first step". He started by following a woman without her knowing it, then getting closer each time. He would masturbate to the fantasies of what he could have done each time, which served to reinforce his growing need to escalate. Ross rationalised this was harmless, a game. This first act was followed by a steady escalation involving grabbing the potential victim, then forcing her into woods, then along a route away from people and getting close to raping before hearing voices and running away. When Ross eventually raped and killed, it was only inevitable because he was ashamed of his fantasies and deeds already and couldn't have told anyone what he was experiencing without opening-up himself to embarrassment or worse.

I depart from the opinion that Ross couldn't control himself. I also believe that forced oral sex, sodomy and rape were all about sexual dominance for him and that murder was the ultimate (deluded) confirmation of his power and potency, and his revenge. He was hugely reinforced by the whole sequence of events, including the stalking, the capture, the brief power of being in complete control and successfully forcing a woman to his will, the raping and the killing.

Killing as a logical next step

I believe also that, for Ross, killing was the logical thing to do to keep himself from capture and punishment. He was a most careful abductor, choosing secluded places and women he didn't know and who didn't know him. He was mentally competent sufficient to get away with it several times. I do not subscribe to the popular American rationalisation that his behaviour is the fault of his, somehow separate, "monster", or that his responsibility was significantly diminished due to "mental illness". There are far too many instances of trials of American murderers and serial killers being mitigated or prosecutions becoming unsuccessful due to the acceptance of mental-illness as grounds for diminished responsibility. Michael Bruce Ross knew what he was doing at every stage of the period of killing. He also knew what he was doing for the next nearly 20 years of his life of prison-based false contrition and savouring notoriety.

As horrific as the eight murders were, in some ways the worst of Ross was evident during an earlier attack and rape in which the victim lived to record her account. What makes this case particularly sickening is that he attacked, raped, brutalised and nearly strangled the woman while her child was with her and, at one point according to Ross, he threatened the mother, "If you don't do what I want, I'll smash the baby's head against the house."

And: "If you look up, I'll kill the baby."

And: "I raped and strangled her and left the mother for dead, with the baby at her side. The baby was trying to suckle—what I thought to be—her mother's dead breast."

The mother was unconscious after being strangled by Ross and left for dead, with the baby lying unprotected beside her.

I struggle to type those words. I try not to imagine what that woman and baby went through. When I force myself to consider Michael Bruce Ross, and the fact that he was allowed to live for nearly 20 years beyond his initial execution date, I remind myself that I have always argued against capital punishment and admired the British for dispensing with it in 1965. As a consequence of having to read accounts of serial killers and contemplating the agonies to which they subjected their victims and the victims' families and other loved ones, I struggle to retain that view. I understand now at a very personal level the argument for the ultimate vengeance, but accept reluctantly it would benefit no-one by adding one more death.

In conclusion

Finally, I would just observe that employing psychiatrists for the defence of a prisoner who is charged with the most serious crimes is a long-established and overwhelmingly American predilection. I wonder how often they would be re-employed in that role should they offer a professional judgement in favour of the prosecution.

What is true of his time in prison is the many appeals and psychiatric assessments which allowed this particular serial killer to live another 18 years, and to make several lawyers significantly richer, before anything resembling justice could finally be done. Contrast that with the quick, horrible deaths his eight innocent victims suffered. Ross lived a life of prurient self-abuse and notoriety for longer than some of his victims lived their own lives. At the end, apparently there were still defence lawyers and many demonstrators still keen to prolong the life of this to my mind contemptible man, who ended so many lives and ruined so many more. Such is American justice.

Michael Bruce Ross was responsible for his crimes. He was mentally aware. His actions were premeditated. Both before, during and after he killed, he knew what he was doing. "Mental-illness" is used in these cases as an attempt to reduce culpability. Torturing and killing people aren't the product of a biological or chemical imbalance in the brain. They are the consequences of deviant, violent thoughts which are the product of abusive events which were both committed by others on the killer and by the killer himself once he was able to act independently. The people who abused him are culpable. The culture which produced his formative values is culpable. And, in the final analysis, he is culpable.

CHAPTER EIGHT
LEVI BELLFIELD: HIDING IN PLAIN SIGHT

Levi Bellfield: Hiding in Plain Sight

Levi Bellfield is a British serial killer. An inconsequential would-be "hard man" who killed three young women and attempted to kill another. The only reason I'm including him in this book is that he is a good example of a type of killer hiding in plain sight and going unchallenged in the face of at least some visibly questionable behaviour.

Bellfield was born and raised in the middle of London and could have been stopped before he became a serial killer if significant others had had the courage and responsibility to report him. He was an inner-city serial killer, who made no attempts to hide his general criminal, bullying life, only his serial killing. And when he was eventually cornered, and the police were in his house asking for him, still it looks as if he was shielded, though whether in complete knowledge of his lethal crimes or simply due to his general criminal lifestyle is something I must leave the reader to ponder.

Bellfield was raised in a part of London not far from the main airport, Heathrow. His family were of Romany or traveller stock and it seems their standards were anti-police and relatively lawless. He grew up surrounded by people who were little more than criminals, and many of whom were actively so, as was Bellfield. He became an overweight, loud, lying, bullying, drug and alcohol bingeing, promiscuous, criminal thug. The promiscuity was the foundation for his worst crimes and, coupled with his belief that he was above the law — based on many years of getting away with it more often than not — he came to believe he lived a charmed life and could offend with impunity.

Childhood and youth

It seems Bellfield's mother was the dominant influence in his child-hood and well into his adult life, but not in a good way. Records of his childhood describe a small "runt" who was a "mummy's boy", with a dominating and controlling parent. It is reasonable to assume that Bell-field's cultural influences mostly involved how to commit crimes of profit without arrest. He gravitated early to a life of heavy drinking, owning or using several cars, working in jobs which allowed him to develop and cultivate his delusional identity as a hard man and womaniser.

By only associating with immature, promiscuous and easily led young women, he deluded himself into thinking he was a woman's man, when in fact he targeted vulnerable teenage girls attending nightclubs, who were getting drunk and, as often as not, probably looking for sex. This is a familiar theme with insecure men. They will approach much younger women, barely beyond being children themselves. The young women tend to have certain common characteristics. They have poorly developed moral codes, seeing sex as natural in relationships, thinking nothing of having several partners, sequentially or contemporaneously, active in a social life centred on groups of friends going to clubs and drinking heavily and/or taking what are now termed recreational drugs. What was once proscribed and outside the norm became recreational.

When Bellfield started having sex with an older woman, at the same time as living full-time with the mother of his two very young children, that person has gone on record as saying his sexual performance was poor, that he would experience failure to ejaculate, and that he was ashamed of his upper body because of the size of his stomach. These aren't the characteristics of a confident, mature adult male. The fact that so many women were prepared to have sex with a man they knew to be married with small children does, however, say something about some peoples' lack of contemporary social morality.

As he grew up in a lawless sub-culture, Bellfield developed into an adolescence where bragging, fighting and drinking, as well as commit-ting crimes regularly, was the landscape. As a young man, he got a job as a nightclub bouncer, where his large size and bullying and intimidating manner allowed him early success in seducing or raping young, inadequate, vulnerable girls.

Impact of early experiences

It is speculation on my part, but one possible source of Bellfield's irrational hatred of, and subsequent targeting of, blonde women might have been the experiences he had aged around 13. It seems he had a crush on a slightly older girl, who by some accounts was his first positive experience with females as an overweight "mummy's boy" being bullied by nearly everyone, according to a childhood friend. All we know beyond that is that this young teenage, blonde girl rejected his advances, that she was murdered, and that the killer wasn't found.

The girl's father received a phone call shortly after her death from what he described as a teenage boy who said, "I'm going to kill you". The father allegedly indicated he felt the caller was Bellfield. If all this was true, it would be significant in Bellfield's formative period as a killer. If, and it is a substantive qualification, the teenage Levi Bellfield was befriended by an attractive, blonde, older girl who went on to become the object of his adolescent desire or, probably in his case, lust, this would have been profoundly significant. The intensity of feelings aroused in this young man would have been indelible. If then she were to reject him, and he had believed her family were advising her away from any contact with him, Bellfield would have been capable of doing her harm. Crucially, if this were the case, we would be seeing the key, trigger event where Bellfield fixated in his mind on irrational hatred for, and resentment of, young blond schoolgirls, especially those who might either reject him or seem to him to be acting superior to himself.

In later life, one of his partners told the police of his twisted appetite for schoolgirls. He used abusive and contemptuous language about them, calling them "dirty little whores" and saying that they all "needed fucking". She recorded that Bellfield tried to make her dress in schoolgirl uniform and, when she refused, he would shout, kick and punch her. At the same time, he also tried to make her use a vibrator on herself while he recorded it. Bellfield lived near an alleyway where he would regularly stalk local schoolgirls as they passed. When she eventually confronted him about this, he confessed he had tried to grab girls and they had been lucky to escape. This is clearly evidence, if true, of a developmental stage in his progression towards rape and murder. Tragically, it seems, for whatever reason an opportunity to stop him in his tracks was missed by people who failed to act on their suspicions.

It would seem he learned his bullying skills early, as a teenager, and had enough success with even younger girls who he targeted, to develop his street talk and manipulative, bullying talents. Of the three women who lived with him and bore him (a total of seven) children, they appear to have been subservient, house-bound, "breeding stock" and sometime victims who were submissive to Bellfield and frightened of him. His final partner said he repeatedly raped her, using her as, in her own words, "target practice". After his arrest, she said she found a bin bag in his shed with "balaclava, knife and a magazine with the faces of blond models scratched out". She said that, although this happened before his arrest, she never went to the police. If true, these are the words of someone who could have acted to prevent crimes. With the benefit of hindsight, it could be argued that she didn't know the magnitude of his crimes and that she was too frightened of Bellfield to go to the police with mere suspicions and some evidence of potential crime materials

With his learned skills in seducing and then subjugating women of relatively low self-esteem and independence, Bellfield was able to create a relatively normal lifestyle. And that is an indictment of contemporary life. It is now accepted that a man can have a number of children with several mothers, be compulsively unfaithful, threatening and violent towards them, and still be allows to live free and unchallenged.

Significant factors and signals

The significance of the "blonde model" information, however, goes to the heart of this serial killer's motivations. It is difficult to escape the impression, having read the details of his longer-term relationships, that there wasn't some element of complicity, or at least moral compromise. Nothing was reported to the police.

Bellfield enjoyed the company of men who shared his tastes for crude and abusive behaviour towards women. This would have served to confirm in his mind that he was accepted and feared, if not admired, by his peers. This perverse fellowship was enhanced by the fact that Bellfield would provide his mates with introductions to young girls who were more than willing to have sex with them.

This sick cycle was further fuelled by Bellfield's ready access to, and use of, illegal drugs, including cocaine and heroin and, perhaps significantly, the date-rape drugs GHB and Rohypnol. Added to this depravity were his arsenal of weapons, including brass knuckles, baseball bats, a machete, samurai sword and, finally, a shotgun. Bellfield lived the life of a modern-day gangster, armed and dangerous. For these years, he was in his element. Crucially, this extended period served to create in his own mind a sense of being untouchable, outside the law.

Another possibly contributing factor in Bellfield's serial killing was how he treated his partners. One illustration from Geoffrey Wansell's book, *The Bus Stop Killer,* is a quote from one of his longest serving partner/victims:

> "Usually he would wrap his belt round my throat and choke me and rape me. He would make me do whatever he wanted. I'd be told to 'be a good little slut'. Levi used lit cigarettes on me, beat me with pool cues and ashtrays, threw me down the stairs and even once took a claw hammer to my body."

At what point would you think it might occur to her to either report him to the police or, at least, leave and take the children with her? Years after Bellfield had been locked away, and it was too late to make any difference, she said: "Levi kept on saying 'I hate blonds, I hate women. You're all c…ts. You're not worth a bolt.'"

There were other significant signals from Bellfield during their time together, some of which if she had reported them to the police would have undoubtedly resulted in his being sent to prison. One of the worst of these was that he bragged that he had raped a disabled girl, lifting her out of her wheelchair and raping her on a car bonnet. Again, arguably and whether what he claimed was true or not, Bellfield might have been stopped or at least investigated before he was.

Staging posts and missed opportunities

These are the staging posts towards his killing. They clearly signal that Bellfield was well on the way, because of his lifestyle, his contempt for women and his particular fetish for and hatred of blondes, towards the cowardly assaults which ended four lives.

But Bellfield *had* come to the notice of the police. Wansell wrote,

> "Indeed by the time that he was finally arrested for the murder of Amelie Delagrange in November 2004 the police criminal records files showed that he had attracted the attention of the Metropolitan Police's officers on no fewer that ninety-two separate occasions…"

He went on to say these records included offences of possession of offensive weapons, possession of stolen vehicles, burglary, theft, assault causing bodily harm, and accusations of rape. Incredibly, Bellfield didn't have the custodial sentences to match.

As Wansell remarks, perhaps the most damning entry in this chronicle of "missed opportunities" are the charges of abduction and false imprisonment of Anna-Maria Rennie, aged 17, in October 2001, and of the attempted murder of Irma Dragoshi, 39, in December 2003. The jury failed to reach verdicts on either of these charges. Remember, Bellfield probably killed Milly Dowler in March 2002, Marsha McDonnell in February 2003, and Amelie Delagrange in August 2004. The implications are clear.

I won't describe the process of arrest, trial and conviction because they don't add to our consideration of the psychology of this serial killer, except to mention that, when the police were finally sent to arrest Bellfield, he was found, eventually, hiding naked under some insulation material in the loft of his home. His partner at the time had initially told investigators he was not there. It was when the officer returned to ask again, explaining the seriousness of the charges, that she told him where Bellfield was.

When convicted, Bellfield was given life imprisonment (with a whole life tariff), which he is serving at the time of writing. He changed his name to Yusuf Rahim in prison. I am reliably informed by someone who used to be a prison officer where he is held that Bellfield did this in order to improve his conditions in prison, because Muslims allegedly enjoy better ones such as greater meal selection, more time off work for religious purposes, etc. Whether this is true or not, if it is true it's no surprise. This person has spent his entire life exploiting and abusing and I have no reason to believe that will change. As he is relatively young, born in 1968, he may still despite his whole life tariff harbour ambitions to one day be released. Let us hope this never happens.

Psychology

So why is Levi Bellfield included in a book about the psychology of serial killers? Because he was born into a criminal sub-culture in one of the world's great cities. He was raised to disrespect the law and take whatever advantage he could of others, including through crime. Also, his hatred of a particular type of person — young, attractive blonde women who he sensed were superior to him. His entire adult life was devoted to crime, violence, bullying, raping and threatening people including whoever was his unfortunate partner, and rendering them morally impotent. Trying to convince himself that he was superior to women such that he could constantly, unrelentingly, verbally and physically abuse and attack them. He is said to have committed hundreds of crimes which went unpunished. Committed dozens of serious crimes which were leniently punished or not punished at all. Stalking and terrorising many women. Attacking and killing at least three of them and attacking at least two others, and probably attacking and possibly killing more.

All of this time he lived freely and in plain view on the outskirts of London. How many people knew about crimes that Bellfield committed and did nothing, including rape and murder? What kind of society are we? Although the theme of this book is an indictment of the sicker strands of American life, this serial killer was entirely a product of a British life, but fortunately not one of the mainstream overwhelming majority. Tragically, his life played out in plain view and no-one stopped him until it was far too late.

CHAPTER NINE
AILEEN WOURNOS: A PROSTITUTE'S REVENGE

CHAPTER NINE

Aileen Wournos: A Prostitute's Revenge

"I robbed them and I killed them as cold as ice, and I would do it again...because I've hated humans for a long time."

Seven men were shot dead in less than one year. When Aileen Wournos confessed to her murders, she claimed her victims had tried to rape her and she killed them in self-defence. But she is eventually recorded as saying, "I'm as guilty as can be, and there's more... I'm a serial killer. I want to come clean and tell the world I killed those men first degree. Robbed and killed them to keep from any witnesses."

Wournos' story has been told many times. She has attracted so much attention as the most notorious American female serial killer that you would think there is little more to say. But shall we take a fresh look from the perspective of the prostitute wronged? The whore abused? Sympathy for the devil as victim?

This woman had a dreadful history of abuse as a child. Her parents were almost still children when they married. Her mother was 14; her father 16. The marriage was a disaster. Her mother divorced Aileen's imprisoned father before she was born. Her father was schizophrenic and a child molester who eventually killed himself in prison. Her mother abandoned her and her siblings when Aileen was just four-years-old. How would you describe this as a start in life?

What are the most important things parents provide for their small children? A safe, clean, warm home. Safe in the sense that they are secure and unthreatened. They will care for you, protect you and provide food, clothing, shelter and, crucially, love. A small girl of four abandoned by her mother and father, who presumably she never knew and would not have thrived had she known him: the worst possible start.

Wournos was then raised by her grandparents. She alleges she was raped by an "accomplice" of her grandfather, who had himself sexually assaulted and beaten her. When she was an eleven-year-old schoolgirl, she was already promiscuous, selling herself for sex, drugs or cigarettes. She was pregnant at 14. The litany of sexual and physical abuse by men, especially those in her family, runs through her childhood and adolescence such that, by the time she left what passed for a home, she was prostituting herself and carried a bitterness towards men that would only deepen into a dangerous hatred.

She was thrown out of the home by her grandfather and turned immediately to prostitution whilst living in the woods near her old home. We see from this that she had no childhood. Only a life of fear, abuse and degradation. Her formative years were spent learning that people who were meant to look after her abused her. Learning that she wasn't safe anywhere and that men were bastards who would abuse her if she let them. Learning that she was worthless. Learning that, if she was to survive, she would have to do it the hard way and on her own. This litany of abuse, crime and rejection could only ever have a tragic ending. I submit that the critical elements, the building blocks, for making a serial killer were already in place.

The adult years of Wournos' life passed with a succession of crimes including driving under the influence, disorderly conduct, and firing a pistol from a moving vehicle, until still only 20 years-of-age she managed to catch the eye of a rich, 69-year-old Floridian, who married her. It is difficult to have a positive view of her motives. It was more likely that she cynically seized the opportunity to exploit this wealthy, lonely old man who probably thought he was lucky to have a young, attractive woman want to marry him. It had no positive influence, as she was immediately in fights and confrontations in bars and went to prison for assault. On her release, she assaulted her aged husband, who had to obtain a restraining order against her within weeks of their wedding. Wournos' solution was to leave Florida and her husband and return to Michigan, where within weeks she was again charged with assault. They divorced soon afterwards. The slim chance she might have had of a relatively stable life was extinguished almost before it began. She was living a totally deranged, violent, promiscuous life, much of which was spent in bars drinking and arguing.

This car wreck of a life continued into the 1980s, with a growing crime record including armed robbery, passing forged cheques, theft of a revolver, car theft, resisting arrest and obstruction of justice. Police found two handguns and ammunition in the stolen car she was driving. Incredibly, I could find no record of her being tried, convicted and sentenced for any of these crimes. At this stage, Wournos was beyond help and would I believe only be stopped by imprisonment or death. There remained however an unlikely and hugely significant event, one which was to be both her potential salvation and her downfall.

Love and betrayal

The next crucial event in Wournos' twisted, criminal life happened when she met a woman, Tyria Moore in 1986 and they became lovers. By all accounts this was a period in her life when she finally felt loved, and that could have changed her life for the better except for one thing. Instead of using their relationship to enable them each to turn their lives around, especially Wournos' life, as it seems Moore was living a relatively crimeless life, they lived off Wournos' income as a prostitute—which probably meant she would have felt obliged to continue this even if she'd wanted to stop. Given it was how she chose to make money, it proved to be her downfall and the fatal decision which led to the deaths of eight innocent people. Ultimately, Moore was to become the person who, crucially, helped police charge Wournos, and whose evidence helped convict her. It is consistent with Wournos' life of failure, defeat and murder that the only time she found love, she felt she had been betrayed.

Wournos had previously done other jobs including working in cafés, but she presumably understood that selling her body for sex was the most profitable and easiest way to make money, and that her previous efforts at normal jobs had all failed due to her temper and confrontational behaviour. She would not have worked for any man save the most inoffensive and compliant. It is important to understand that her decision to continue prostituting herself, and to do this by placing herself on the roads and highways, was key in what was to happen, and it was her choice.

Seven victims

The first victim of this serial killer was also to prove critical as a trigger for the rest. Wournos claimed she shot a customer because he raped her, and that it was in self-defence. We will never know the truth. But what I believe we do know is that this triggered something in her which could not be reversed. The victim, Richard Mallory, was a convicted rapist. If we consider whether or not he raped Wournos, why would he have done this when he had paid for consensual sex? Of course, it's possible that he did it because he wanted to rape her and thought he could get away with it. But he didn't realise that he was raping a time-bomb and that he was triggering it. Wournos would have felt exhilaration and release in killing a perceived rapist. She would finally feel the power tables had turned and that she was taking revenge for a lifetime of being sexually abused or raped by men.

The next six killings, all by shooting, took place over less than a year and there was never a repeat of provocation in their circumstances. In fact, Wournos was now out-of-control and a lethal threat to any man who paid her to prostitute herself, regardless of their conduct. Her choice of victims from the customers was, it seems, capricious and we will probably never know if there was a pattern in terms of their behaviour towards her or their appearance.

What, you may ask, of the burden of responsibility as an adult? Many commentators and people involved in Wournos' story have expressed an element of sympathy for her based on her horrible life. It is true she was set upon at a terribly young age by the most dreadful circumstances, and that she never had a chance to live a healthy life. This is a persuasive mitigating argument. Perhaps she should not have been executed because she was as much a victim as an offender. Sadly, I find that I cannot subscribe to this view.

Aileen Wournos was, in my view, vindictive, bitter, uncontrolled, illogical, unstable, violent, alcoholic, predatory, man-hating, egocentric and deeply damaged. The life she lived as a result caused grievous damage. She was a lesbian and a prostitute who hated men and that was never a personal conflict which could be resolved. If it were possible to feel any mitigation, it was after the first killing. It was possible that she retaliated to being sexually assaulted or worse. When she then chose to go on a serial killing spree, she abrogated totally any justification that we might see in her as a victim.

There are many people who experience some, or indeed all, of the terrible events that Wournos did and they don't subsequently live violent criminal lives resulting in serial killing. What she did was not inevitable. It was significantly more likely, but not inevitable. As an adult, she chose to go out prostituting with a gun. She chose to kill men whose only "crime" was to pay her for sex. She did it seven times. She may have had some mitigation the first time. After that, she knew what she was doing, and she was responsible for the consequences.

Wournos was the subject of varied and extensive media attention, including a motion picture. She continues to be one of the most popular serial killers for the media.

Imprisonment

Wournos was tried and convicted in 1992 for the first murder. She was ultimately convicted of six of the seven killings and received the death sentence. Anyone familiar with the American legal system for the death penalty and associated plethora of appeals will know that convictions only serve to begin the next long phase of the convicted person's life. Ten years later, in 2002, she was finally executed. It could be argued that she could have lived in prison for several more years before exhausting the appeal procedures. Apparently she grew tired of life inside and stated:

> "I killed those men. Robbed them as cold as ice. And I'd do it again, too. There's no chance in keeping me alive or anything because I'd kill again. I have hate crawling through my system...I am so sick of hearing this 'she's

crazy' stuff. I've been evaluated so many times. I'm competent, sane, and I'm trying to tell the truth. I'm one who seriously hates human life and would kill again."

I have absolutely no doubt that this confession was true and tells us all we need to know about the real Aileen Wournos. It's just a pity ten years had to pass before she decided to tell the truth to suit her own agenda.

Killing those men was the prostitute's revenge. But the only person responsible for the Aileen Wournos who chose to kill was herself. She didn't have to be a prostitute. She didn't have to operate on isolated highways at night. She didn't have to carry a loaded handgun. She didn't have to shoot anyone. She didn't have to spend ten years costing the taxpayers to keep her alive until she grew tired of prison life.

A cultural post-mortem

The most extraordinary thing about the Wournos story happened after her death. The director of a documentary about her commented, "I think this anger just spilled out from inside her. And finally exploded into incredible violence." I agree with this, but he went on to say,

> "That was her way of surviving. I think Aileen really believed that she had killed in self-defence. I think someone who's deeply psychotic can't really tell the difference between something that is life-threatening and something that is a minor disagreement, that you could say something that she didn't agree with. She would get into a screaming black temper about it… *and at the same time, when she wasn't in those extreme moods, there was an incredible humanity to her.*"

Critically though:

- killing men who were paying her for sex wasn't a way of surviving. It was a way of killing innocent people
- she didn't kill in self-defence and she didn't think that she had

- she wasn't "deeply psychotic" in my opinion because I found nothing in records or reports to suggest she had completely lost contact with the reality in which she found herself. She knew she was in prison and was facing the death penalty; and
- saying that a serial killer had an incredible humanity when she wasn't killing is like describing a fundamentalist terrorist as a religious role model.

Popular culture

Wikipedia has a segment of its entry on Wournos entitled "In popular culture". There her entry lists the many books, documentaries, films, an opera(!), and several songs about her. They finish by referring to a singer called Diamanda Galas, who apparently performed a cover version of a song "Iron Lady" as "a tribute" to Wournos.

How does the great American public react to male serial killers who had terrible lives, who were raped or otherwise sexually abused, beaten, rejected, etc. and who went on to kill women? This gender-based hypocrisy. Am I alone in questioning the health and judgement of "popular culture" in making her a famous victim? She was a lifelong violent criminal who killed seven people out of a sense of outraged grievance. They are the victims, not her.

Interviewed on the day before her execution, Wournos accused the police of having been able to arrest her after her first murder as she'd left prints everywhere. However, she then proceeded to unravel in an increasingly angry and irrational rant full of persecutory and grandiose delusions. Apparently having been diagnosed as mentally fit to be executed, it is impossible to determine whether she was faking illness or genuinely unstable. Too late. What is indisputable is how emotionally brittle, bitter and uncontrollably angry she continued to be even unto the end, and how twisted.

CHAPTER TEN
PAUL BERNARDO AND KARLA HOMOLKA: A COUPLE IN CANADA

CHAPTER TEN

Paul Bernardo and Karla Homolka:
A Couple in Canada

This chapter focuses on two serial killers who as their relationship progressed married one another. Paul Bernardo and Karla Homolka together enacted one of the most horrific familial atrocities I have ever known. Although Bernardo was eventually convicted of torture, sexual assault, rape and murder, by my calculation it may have been Homolka who was sometimes instrumental if not the "Lady Macbeth" of their killing spree.[1] Yet, thanks to a pre-emptive offer of a plea bargain from prosecutors, she was charged and convicted only of manslaughter, and given a relatively light sentence of 12 years. This was on condition that she gave evidence against Bernardo. She was also, during much of their appalling period of crimes, both a victim of violence from Bernardo and an active participant in his crimes. The two are not antithetical.

The evil of these two, and that which sets them apart from even the sordid realities of other serial killers, is what they did to Homolka's sister, Tammy. Another unusual aspect is that the killers did not appear to have the trigger experience characteristic of serial killers.

There are several decisions made in this case which, I will argue, from a lay perspective as I am not a lawyer, appear to be examples of poor judgement or extraordinary ineptitude.

---

1.   As with other cases in this book I stress that this is my interpretation after studying the available materials. Here in particular readers should note that Homolka (who now lives in the community under an assumed name) is actively, if controversially, seeking a governmental pardon, on the basis it would seem that her will was subjugated to Bernardo and his threats.

Bernardo's formative influences

Paul Bernardo had the kind of childhood which goes some way to explaining his attitudes to women and sex. Tragically, he had a mother who conceived him due to adultery. When she eventually confessed this to him, his view of her is recorded as one of contempt, calling her a "slob" and a "whore". The man he thought was his father was abusive to his wife and children, and was charged with sexually abusing a female child, and, according to one account, he sexually abused his own daughter. He was also reported to have been caught peeping into the windows of young women.

Bernardo's mother Marilyn was suffering from depression, becoming morbidly obese and withdrawn from the family. She neglected the children and is described as having withdrawn emotionally and physically, isolating herself in the basement for much of her time. It is reasonable to assume these facts would have had a formative influence on Paul. I suggest he formed strong feelings of contempt for her and shame for his "father", the man who had adopted him and given him his name. This is not a loving, nurturing childhood. We know nothing of how his older siblings grew-up in such a dysfunctional home.

Despite these abusive influences, young Bernardo seems to have developed many positive attributes, including being popular, friendly and well-mannered. He was active in the Boy Scouts, and there are accounts of him working hard in after school jobs, being popular, well-liked, and doing well in school. The effects of his mother's confession of infidelity and her descent into depression, withdrawal and obesity are significant, as would have been having a sex abuser as a stepfather.

At some point in late adolescence, it seems Bernardo developed more hostile attitudes towards women. He was described as having "developed dark sexual fantasies, enjoyed humiliating women in public" and would beat-up women he dated. I struggle to understand how this development occurred, except that he must have harboured bitter unresolved feelings of betrayal from his mother, and found that, because he was attractive and popular with young women, he could have his way with them, especially sexually. If his early experiences of being aggressive and dominant were rewarded with sexual gratification and a sense of power, it would have significantly strengthened his learning and he would have wanted more.

Bernardo inherited no healthy, internalised moral values from his family. He had been associating with other adolescent boys who were aggressive, bragging petty criminals. The gradual descent towards rape was in place.

It is important to understand that the learning necessary to move from aggressive but consensual sex to rape can be small, even imperceptible, in the mind of the rapist. It is important to record that Bernardo committed at least two rapes and an attempted rape before he met Homolka, so he was already a rapist. Crucially, he was a "successful" rapist in that he got away with it. A few months after his first known rape, he met Homolka. I believe this fact was crucial in the events that followed. I quote from a passage at the Murderpedia website:

> "In October 1987, he met Karla Homolka. They became sexually interested in each other almost immediately. Unlike the other girls he knew, she encouraged his sadistic sexual behaviour, also encouraging his acts as the 'Scarborough Rapist.'"

Bernardo later claimed that he had committed at least 30 rapes. It follows that most of these happened when they were together and that she would have both known about them and presumably encouraged them. The part she played in these brutal sexual assaults was vital and appalling. Bernardo was a serial rapist before he was a serial killer. He then combined these two atrocities to horrific effect, actively encouraged, aided and abetted by Homolka. She was, in my view, as guilty as he was. In one particularly sick and brutal series of events involving her sister, Homolka plumbed the depths of human sibling depravity.

Karla Homolka

While it is possible to see the experiences and drives which contributed to the creation of Paul Bernardo, serial killer, his active accomplice (which, of course, she denies being) is far more challenging. In my efforts to research her life, especially her childhood and adolescence, what I found was extraordinary. Apparently, her life "began" when she met Bernardo. Unlike the other killers researched, there was nothing on her life before then. Her Wikipedia entry only refers to her life with him, as if the previous 17 years didn't exist. On Murderpedia, her life before Bernardo was worthy of four sentences, while subsequent book, movie and TV programmes only address her as his active accomplice, and her life after Bernardo. This unique treatment of a serial offender speaks volumes about cultural gender prejudices. The subconscious presumption is that Homolka didn't exist before she came under Bernardo's influence; that there is no significance to her early life relevant to a better understanding of how she came to be what she was. We are in effect asked to assume there is no interest in her life before then, when in fact Homolka was probably the more intelligent—and arguably the more manipulative and cunning—of the pair. Where was her moral compass? Although it's a dreadfully well-trodden field, I am obliged to briefly outline what Homolka did for her to be the subject of so much inattention.

Between 1987 and 1992, Karla Homolka:

- encouraged and supported Bernardo in sadistic sexual behaviour, much of it directed towards her
- encouraged him in some of his series of rapes which earned him the label "The Scarborough Rapist", of which he was proud
- procured a 15-year-old girl to be Bernardo's latest rape victim, who she is said to have drugged and plied with alcohol. Homolka then raped the girl before offering her to Bernardo as his "surprise wedding gift" from her. The girl almost died as a result of the cocktail of alcohol and drugs Homolka seemingly gave her.
- with Bernardo she videotaped their atrocities
- repeated the procedure of procurement via drugs on *her own* 15-year-old sister (see below)
- participated in the further activities described below.

Because Bernardo was sexually attracted to Homolka's sister Tammy, Homolka premeditated a plan to drug her sister and offer her to Bernardo as her Christmas gift. The level of moral depravity necessary to behave like that is truly extremely difficult to countenance. The pair filmed themselves as they raped Tammy in the basement of Bernardo's parents' house. Although it was recorded as unintended, Tammy died after choking on her own vomit. The two depraved individuals then attempted to cover-up their deeds before ringing the emergency services. Despite significant culpatory evidence, the coroner recorded a verdict of accidental death.

The greatest depravity, however, remained. Sometime later, Homolka dressed-up in her dead sister's clothes, pretended to be Tammy, had sex with Bernardo, and they filmed themselves doing it. There are no words sufficient to adequately describe a young woman who is capable of drugging her own little sister in order to allow her fiancé to rape her, to then film it, contribute directly to her sister's death and cover it up. Finally, to dress in her dead sister's clothes, parade provocatively in front of her rapist/killer husband to be, and then have sex so dressed. I have never encountered this level of filial depravity before and struggle to even attempt to explain it.

In June 1991, Homolka and Bernardo tortured and raped a 14-year-old girl who Bernardo had abducted. The girl had attended a funeral, missed her curfew and been locked out of her home. Homolka actively and voluntarily participated in this prolonged sexual torture and assault and, according to Barnardo, it was she who fed the victim a lethal dose of Halcion, a drug she took from a veterinary surgery where she worked. Homolka was actively involved in equal measure in the disposal of the poor victim's body.

Homolka, while driving around with Bernardo looking for new victims, distracted their next victim until Bernardo could threaten her with a knife and force her into the car. This girl too was brutalised in similar fashion. Seemingly, Bernardo always intended to kill the girl as they had made no attempt to conceal their identifies from their victim. After several days of the police failing to find either the missing victim or her killers, another young woman who had previously been stalked by Bernardo told police she had spotted him, but the police mishandled her report, negating any chance of the girl's body being found in Bernardo's house.

There's more, but it is sufficient to conclude that Homolka was so far as I can tell an enthusiastic and equally culpable partner in their many horrible crimes. She may have been the instigator on occasions and encouraged Bernardo's depravity as well as embellishing the atrocities with her own uniquely sordid and degenerate acts. This view is confirmed by both the evidence during their trials and the videotapes of some of their crimes.

I feel obliged to try and explain how this young woman could have behaved in this way. She had by all accounts a normal and stable upbringing and there is nothing to suggest developmental crises or influences towards such extreme pathology. Obviously, because he was six years older and a dominant influence in sadistic acts, it has to be accepted that Bernardo was a significant influence, but if you have been raised to have a social conscience, to care about others and to love and protect your family, especially a younger sister, how can such involvement be explained?

Sadly, I assume Homolka enjoyed the sex with Bernardo, which would have reinforced these deviant acts. Equally, if she thought she loved him and was going to marry him, and she knew that procuring young girls as sexual objects could result in his pleasure, then this would strengthen their bond and enhance her influence over him. If she had only weakly developed morals, and was immature in her life experiences, then the influence over her that Bernardo held through his bullying and subjugation would have created in her the belief that what they were doing was exciting and dangerous. There was also a degree of cooperation by more than one of their victims in so far as they returned and repeated some of the sexual acts. But Homolka must have known that Bernardo was raping repeatedly and she did nothing to prevent it or report it, so was enabling his rapes.

Attempts to arrest and prosecute

I want to list some of the facts pertaining to attempts to arrest, convict and punish the pair:

- another man, Robert Baltovich, despite consistently protesting his innocence, was convicted of the second-degree murder of his girlfriend, one of Bernardo's victims. Baltovich was innocent. He served eight years of a life sentence before being released pending his appeal. It took another four years before that appeal was heard, when his conviction was "set aside" in December 2004. Seven months later, the Attorney General of Ontario announced a new trial. Nearly three more years passed before the prosecutor announced he would call no new evidence and asked the jury to find Baltovich not guilty. So, it took the relevant authorities 16 years, half of which involved locking-up an innocent man in prison for murder, and then declining to pursue what was obviously a wrongful conviction. I found no record of an apology. It is to be hoped that Baltovich sued.
- a further man, Anthony Hanemaayer, was wrongfully convicted of a sexual assault Bernardo committed in 1989. He served a 16 months prison sentence and was "exonerated" only after Bernardo admitted the crime 27 years later.
- in 1996, a report into police mishandling of the Bernardo case reported, acknowledging among other things that the police had "mishandled" vital witness information which might have led to saving lives, including that of one of the girls that Bernardo subsequently killed
- in spite of having questioned Bernardo several times concerning the Scarborough Rapist investigation, and people reporting Bernardo as suspected of being the person they were looking for, and in spite of having a DNA-sample from Bernardo which would have directly linked him to the crimes, police were not informed that it matched Barnardo for another 26 months!

Incredibly, when they were shown this proof, they still failed to arrest him, only placing him under "24-hour surveillance".

- critically, police delayed arresting Bernardo until after Homolka. Following a vicious physical beating by Bernardo, she obtained the services of a lawyer who asked for immunity from prosecution for Homolka in exchange for her giving evidence against Bernardo. She was offered a significantly reduced sentence of 12 years' imprisonment (which seems to have happened after the prosecutor viewed videotapes of some of the rapes in which she had played an active part!). She was told that, if she declined, she risked being charged with two counts of first-degree murder, one of second-degree murder, and other crimes. Are we to conclude from this that prosecutors, knowing the nature of her crimes to the extent that they did were content to offer Homolka a 12-year sentence in order to improve their chance of convicting Bernardo? Is this justice in action?

- For what seem to me to be questionable "legal reasons" Bernardo's original defence lawyer took possession of videotapes depicting rapes and assaults. Prosecutors said that they would never have agreed to Homolka's plea bargain had they seen them and the extent of their contents (one lawyer it should be stressed was later acquitted of obstructing justice).

Fear of litigation would cause someone to pause before asserting police incompetence, but it seems there are women who would be alive today, and women who would not have been raped, had they acted sooner. Equally, it might be argued that, but for legal tactics, Homolka would have received sentences more proportionate to her crimes and, like Bernardo, would have been imprisoned for longer. This type of after-the-fact judgemental speculation can be criticised, but which is the greater harm?

Cynical exploitation

Perhaps inevitably, given the nature of the commercial potential in exploiting horror, there has been a film, several TV programmes and the "usual suspects" cashing in on the notoriety of this case. Bernardo himself managed to produce and self-publish in 2015 a "violent, fictional, 631-page e-book" entitled "A MAD World Order". In two weeks, it is recorded to have become an Amazon bestseller, "but was quietly removed from that website due to a public outcry". My only surprise is that there wasn't an even greater outcry from those deprived of their need to feed on this "garbage".

The psychology of Bernardo and Homolka

Paul Bernardo was a rapacious sexual predator whose primary aim was to gratify his increasingly perverted sexual fantasies. He killed to destroy the risk of his victims becoming prosecution witnesses. Serial killers like Bernardo play into the hands of those who favour capital punishment. He should be grateful for Canada's relatively lenient laws which allow him to live in relative comfort and the hope that one day he, unlike his victims, will be free to live his life.

It is, indeed, informative to mention Bernardo's more current life and attempts to gain release on parole. In an account from a local Canadian newspaper of his most recent Parole Board review, Bernardo was full of psychological jargon and conspicuously little transparency. Apart from the mention of a "romantic relationship" in 2014 during which, he told the psychologist reporting, of his increased fantasies about dominant sexual acts including anal sex, and increased masturbation, Bernardo was also said to have shown "minimal gains" from the three treatment courses, one for sex offenders, he'd completed in prison.

The trial judge recorded that he felt Bernardo required imprisonment for the rest of his life. After 25 years, the Parole Board said he has "a high risk for intimate partner violence". There are two aspects to the British prison system's parole release considerations: tariff and risk. Has the offender served sufficient time commensurate with the seriousness of the crime (their basic tariff to be served before parole can be considered), and what risk is he or she to the public if released? On both counts, for me, Bernardo should never be released.

Karla Homolka was an impressionable, initially submissive, sex object for Bernardo who grew to enjoy their complicitous sexual deviancy and violent subjugation of young girls. Early in their relationship, she was part victim, part provider. As time passed and she enjoyed her growing influence and power, she seemingly became a more enthusiastic, morally compromised, accomplice to Bernardo. When they were facing trial and prison, she acted to ensure she was dealt with far more leniently than I believe her actions deserved and did not hesitate to provide authorities with everything she knew about Bernardo's crimes, so long as it served her purpose. I cannot understand why Homolka's evidence was so critical, or why she was not charged and convicted of far more serious crimes for which she should have been given a life sentence, which she should still be serving.

CHAPTER ELEVEN
STEPHEN GRIFFITHS: THE CROSSBOW CANNIBAL

Stephen Griffiths: The Crossbow Cannibal

S tephen Griffiths is from Yorkshire, England. He killed three women between 2009 and 2010. In the obscene hierarchy of serial killers, he had relatively few victims and received comparatively little media attention. This will disappoint him, as according to reports of his own assertions the only thing he really wanted was to become one of the most infamous serial killers. In that he failed. I include his story here to draw attention to the extent to which a descent into malign, pornographic, isolation can happen in the middle of a normal active life in a city where people are either oblivious to what is happening near them or choose not to do what would seem to be the morally right thing. This in order to either profit or from other base motives.

An unusual killer

Griffiths is an unusual serial killer in many respects. He didn't kill, in my view, out of a malign hatred of the victims or type of victim. He wasn't struggling and failing to control his sexual urges, either as a closet homosexual or sexual sadist. He hadn't fixated on a specific object of hatred such as Levi Bellfield (*Chapter Eight*), Ted Bundy (*Chapter Thirteen*) or others in this book did. He simply wanted more than anything else in this world to become famous, or preferably infamous, as a serial killer.

The interesting thing about this otherwise relatively inconsequential individual was the extremes to which he was prepared to go in order to create an alter-ego to be feared. The story of his transformation from Stephen Griffiths, insignificant loner, to "Ven Pariah", serial killer, is the account of a trajectory which goes some way to aiding our understanding of this dysfunctional type of killer.

Upbringing and progression to violent offending

There is relatively little information on Griffiths' childhood to suggest what he would one day become. It was by all accounts relatively stable until his parents divorced when he was quite young. Record has it that he blamed his mother for this split and was reported to have had "utter contempt for her." It was also reported that she may have been a prostitute and that she had on occasion gone about the garden of their house naked in the company of other men. I would view this as unconfirmed, at least going on what I've been able to find on the subject. But, if it were true, then these events would have had a much more significant effect on the young Griffiths than would be thought. He would have had a low opinion of his mother and possibly have hated her, and arguably she would have been an exceptionally poor parent.

His father saved-up enough money to send Griffiths to a private school. Unfortunately, his behaviour was poor, and he failed to last there. In his early teenage years, he developed a morbid fascination with John Haigh, labelled the Acid Bath Murderer, an infamous British serial killer of the 1940s who dissolved his victim's bodies in chemicals in his London workshop. Griffiths also developed a morbid fascination with killing generally, and serial killing specifically. He was intelligent, but dysfunctional socially, which was already serving to isolate him from any stabilising or controlling influence on the direction his life was taking.

In 1987, aged 18, he went into a shop to steal. He was caught red-handed and attacked the shop worker with a knife, inflicting a wound on his neck which required 16 stitches. For this vicious assault, he was sent to custody for three years. During his time inside, Griffiths told a probation officer that he fantasised about becoming a serial killer. Apparently, this was dismissed as "bravado". It was to remain a signal, a warning unheeded. He would have served only 18 months of his sentence if his behaviour inside hadn't warranted concern resulting in loss of remission.

Not long after his release, Griffiths was convicted of possessing an air pistol. I couldn't find any reference to what punishment he received. In 1991, he was diagnosed by a psychiatrist as a "sadistic, schizoid psychopath". The label of schizoid psychopath describes someone having:

> "Pervasive emotional detachment, reduced affect, lack of close friends, apathy, anhedonia, insensitive to social norms, asexuality, preoccupation with fantasy, autistic thinking without loss of skill to recognise reality."

This condition isn't treatable within the Royal College of Psychiatrists (RCP) guidelines but Griffiths certainly had most of these characteristics, particularly preoccupation (I would say obsession) with fantasy, and emotional detachment. Anhedonia is an inability to find pleasure in normally pleasurable activities. I couldn't say whether this was true of Griffiths or not.

In 1992, he received a two-year prison sentence for affray and possession of an offensive weapon after holding a knife to the throat of a young girl for no apparent reason. He was seen regularly during his teenage years by psychiatrists. He told them of his "compulsion to kill", but I could find no record of action to address or treat this. A number of contradictory conclusions made by psychiatrists and psychologist range from "not mentally-ill" to "complex and untreatable personality disorder". What I think was being implied was the subtle distinction psychiatrists make between a diagnosis of a treatable condition under the Mental Health Act, and psychopathy, which is generally held to be untreatable. The difference in terms of aberrant behaviour however could be argued as a matter of different but comparable disorders of personality.

Griffith was sectioned at one point as a patient at Rampton Secure Hospital, where psychiatrists recorded variously that he was not mentally-ill, not suitable for treatment, had a severe personality disorder, was dangerous, and was a schizoid psychopath. The effect of these various and somewhat disparate diagnoses was that he did not fall within the remit of a psychiatric label which was treatable and was released. This in spite of an interesting personal history including being a "Satanist, possessing terrorist knives [there were 30 in his flat]... lifelong use of knives with several knife-related convictions"; also being totally obsessed with killing, with a history of knifing a man for which he served three years in prison and of threatening women with knives to their faces.

It is difficult to understand what could have been done to intervene in the life of this obviously unstable and dangerous young man sufficient to provide some safeguard to the public. I haven't had access to the records from Rampton, but it would be interesting to see if there were any acknowledgements of the risk he posed.

In 1993, Griffiths was put on probation for possessing a knife in public and given a suspended prison sentence for possessing two air pistols.

University and more violent behaviour

In the autumn of 1997, Griffiths began studying for his BA degree at Leeds University. In 1998, he dated a woman for two years, but the relationship is reported to have broken down when he invited her back to his flat, where she saw a large number of knives, crossbows, a substantial collection of pornographic material, and that all the furniture was covered in plastic sheets. He is said to have dated one other woman after this, but this relationship also failed, following the miscarriage of what is reported to have been his child and his abusive behaviour towards her.

On another occasion, Griffiths was found not guilty of pouring boiling water on, and badly burning, a sleeping girlfriend who had decided to leave him. There are reports too of other girlfriends going to the police but not being prepared to testify in court for fear of retaliation. Another girlfriend is recorded to have had her legs cut by Griffiths with broken glass and to have had her nose broken and been knocked out by him. When she left him, he was given a court order to stay away from her, but he broke that by slashing the tyres of her car and painting graffiti on her apartment wall. For these actions he was convicted of harassment.

By 2001, Griffiths had begun to drink heavily and take drugs. He bought two large lizards and took them for walks on dog leads, cultivating an increasingly menacing appearance which featured leather clothes and slicked back hair. Apparently, to his undoubted disappointment, he wasn't taken seriously as either menacing or threatening. There are reports from neighbours or others who saw him of extreme behaviours like feeding live rats to his lizards and, extraordinarily, one of seeing him eat a live rat!

Being now unemployed, Griffiths was spending more and more time accessing pornography and violence on the internet and pursuing his growing interest in serial killers. He had obtained his BA in 2003, so was still functioning at a relatively impressive intellectual level even if his darker side was growing more malign. He was by this time increasingly withdrawn, a classic feature of the pathology whereby he was able to nurture and develop his malevolent life view without challenge.

The following year, in 2004, he was accepted onto a PhD research programme at Bradford University. His thesis was entitled "Homicide in an Industrial City—Violence in Bradford 1847-1899". What he was really studying, in my opinion, was serial killers. It is difficult now to reflect on how a man with his history of mental illness and violent crime would not have been scrutinised more carefully as to his suitability for such study and for being accepted onto a post-graduate course which would allow him to indulge his growing obsession, with official academic sanction. For the next six years, Griffiths studied killing on this part-time course until he put all that he had learned into practice.

The *Yorkshire Post* records that during his period of study at Bradford, Griffiths had little contact with staff or fellow students. His research involved searching through the archives of newspapers and periodicals at Bradford City Library. His work was under the supervision of Bradford's School of Lifelong Learning and Development, apparently costing up to £1,740 a year in fees.

He is recorded as having been disciplined for threatening fellow students after losing his temper during seminars. It can only be speculative, but, from autumn 2004 when he began the course in Bradford and January 2009 when he was given a conditional discharge for harassment, it is reasonable to assume that he was becoming increasingly detached from any chance of living a relatively normal life and was feeding his growing perversions. During this period, he created an alter ego, a persona which he labelled "Ven Pariah", apparently after an obscure fantasy figure from demonology. In researching Griffiths, I discovered one of the best articles on him, and sadly also one of the few to display any intellectual rigour. Theodore Dalrymple, a former doctor and prison psychiatrist, wrote "Murder Most Academic" for the *City Journal Magazine* (a publication of the Manhattan Institute for Policy Research, New York), in December 2010. The following is an extract:

> "Sometimes reality is far in advance of satire when it comes to absurdity. The results, however, are not always funny. If a satirist had come up with the idea of a violent criminal who had spent time in an asylum being admitted by a university to its doctoral program in 'homicide studies', thereafter turning into a serial killer, that satirist would have been denounced for poor taste. But this is precisely what a British university did recently. A man with a long history of criminal violence became a serial killer while working on a PhD thesis at the University of Bradford, the subject of his thesis being the methods of homicide used in the city during the nineteenth century."

Dalrymple went on to explain that to add to "their fascinating chronicle of acceptance", the university, when contacted on the question of Griffiths continuing his studies after conviction for serial killing, said via a spokeswoman that his was an unusual case and Griffiths would have to apply to the university to continue. He had not done so, but if he did they would have to look at the university's regulations. "An unusual case!" gasps Dalrymple, "the mind boggles", concluding that the clear implication was that should this convicted serial killer wish to apply to continue his doctoral studies, then the university, "in its wisdom, would consider his application consistent with their regulations." What, wonders Dalrymple would Griffiths have to do to forfeit that right!

Dalrymple's castigates a piece in the *Guardian* ("'Crossbow cannibal' victims' drug habits made them vulnerable to violence", 21 December 2010). His view is that this article was saying (paraphrased) "people who suffer or have led unhappy lives must be transformed into blameless victims so we can pity them." Delivering an extended rebuke to this "liberal" take on prostitutes he recounts having, in his career as a medical doctor, had many patients who were prostitutes and cites the case of one who lived a successful life, including raising her daughter well, saying "Neither she nor any other prostitute whom I met claimed to have been driven onto the streets by anything other than their own mistakes". In other words Stephen Griffiths not his victims or their way of life was responsible for his behaviour towards rhem.

Ven Pariah "Bloodbath Artist"

Between June 2009 and May 2010, Griffiths killed three women who were working as prostitutes in the area where he lived, the Red Light District of Bradford, having chosen to live there deliberately. These women were vulnerable and had no realistic way of protecting themselves against an unstable murderous man determined to kill them and armed with a crossbow. In all of this, Griffiths was a coward. He needed to inhabit the persona of his malevolent alter-ego Ven Pariah, as Stephen Griffiths would have been inadequate to commit even these cowardly deeds. It is not my intention to provide gratuitous pleasure by describing them. My purpose is to attempt to explain the psychology of this serial killer and the cultural moral perfidy of some of those who either failed to act or who only acted responsibly after attempting to profit from their information.

After his second murder, Griffiths recorded a video on his mobile phone. He lost the phone on a train. Someone picked it up, watched the video, and then apparently sold the phone so that others could watch an actual murder added to which Griffiths had recorded a narrative, stating "I am Ven Pariah. I am the Bloodbath Artist." And Griffiths had spray painted "My sex slave" on the victim's body. Disgusting. The phone was sold again before it came into the hands of the police. I don't know how many people saw the recording and failed to notify the police, but it is a sad indictment of those peoples' morals.

Police had been aware of Griffith's menace as they had previously confiscated hunting weapons and knew his criminal history. They had agreed with the housing association that surveillance was needed. Because of concerns about his behaviour, better CCTV had been installed to scan the hallway outside his flat. The third and final murder was partially recorded on this, along with Griffith's returning to the camera after killing, his crossbow still in one hand, as he proceeded to make an offensive one fingered gesture towards the camera. This pathetic act was consistent with his new persona and would have been felt by him as strong and defiant. An employee at the flats saw this footage when routinely reviewing recordings. His next act wasn't to notify the police, but to ring the *Sun* newspaper to try to sell the story. Yet another morally impoverished act and, sadly, no longer surprising.

Stephen Griffiths realised his nightmare. For years, he had been fantasising about becoming an infamous serial killer. He knew he had to be different, and menacing. He knew he had to meet the definition of serial killing "two or more" people over time, i.e. not in a single act (*Chapter One*). He knew he needed to publicise what he did for maximum effect.

Taken together, there was more than enough information about this isolated dangerous loner to see the risk. There must have been questions too about the judgement displayed in accepting him to study murder and serial killing given his history, behaviour and lifestyle. Was there really nothing that could have been done to prevent these tragic killings? Are we so detached and quick to wash our hands? What hope is there that another Stephen Griffiths isn't already among us?

CHAPTER TWELVE
GARY RIDGWAY: THE GREEN RIVER KILLER

Gary Ridgway: The Green River Killer

G ary Ridgway is another American serial killer. His claim to infamy is that he is the second most prolific known serial killer in American history, having recently been replaced at the top of the macabre list by Samuel Little (see *Chapter Five*). I include a chapter on Ridgway in order to explore two aspects of the phenomenon more closely: the absence of personality in the offender; and the related obsession with killing as many people as possible, specifically in order to become famous (compare, e.g. Stephen Griffiths in *Chapter Eleven*). Apart from Ted Bundy, who I deal with next, and Eileen Wournos (*Chapter Nine*), there has been more media attention for this individual serial killer than almost any other. But he really is "nothing" apart from his crime.

Ridgeway's upbringing

Ridgway was born in 1949 in Utah. He had a not untypical, dysfunctional American family, with rowing parents, including a domineering mother who introduced him, in my opinion, to sexual conflict by her parenting. Wikipedia tells us that his childhood also featured chronic bed-wetting which meant that his mother "would wash his genitals after every episode." You might think this response would encourage more wetting rather than discourage it, given the family dynamics. The article goes on to report that "as an adolescent, he had conflicting feelings of anger and sexual attraction toward his mother and fantasised about killing her." Any self-respecting psychodynamic psychiatrist or psychotherapist would have a field day with that information! I will content myself by suggesting there may have been a causative link between these experiences and feelings, and his subsequent treatment of prostitutes.

Ridgway contracted gonorrhoea from a prostitute he had sex with. Regarding his many victims, most of whom were prostitutes, he apparently avoided their faces during both sex and killing them. This may have been a form of avoidance because he would have found it too distressing to continue or, more likely, they were objects to him and he approached them to exploit, rape and kill as simply objects of contempt and hatred. I suspect it is insignificant except to note that he tended to strangle his victims from behind.

Curiously Ridgway's first experience of carrying-out a violent attack was to take a six-year-old boy into woods when he himself was only 16, and to stab the child through the ribs. Both Ridgway and the victim are recorded as saying that he walked away saying, "I always wondered what it would be like to kill someone." It would seem this experience was just that, a rehearsal, and a significant staging post in his learning how to kill. Although the method isn't consistent with that he used on his female victims, the casual, callous lack of feelings is.

Sexual obsession and promiscuity

As a young adult, Ridgway eventually graduated from high school aged 20 (it's normally 17; he was forced to repeat a year's study twice). He promptly married his girlfriend, enlisted in the US Navy, was sent to Vietnam, where he saw combat and often had sex with prostitutes. On his discharge, he discovered his wife too had been unfaithful and their marriage ended soon afterwards. This pattern of mutual infidelity continued with his second marriage, which also failed.

The biggest problem seems to have been Ridgway's sexual obsession. By all accounts, from his wives and other women in his life, he had an insatiable sexual appetite. Several women, including his three wives, reported him demanding sex several times a day, and that he enjoyed sex outdoors, either in public places or secluded wooded areas. This is a key feature of this serial killer, and one which sets him apart from most others.

A complicating and, possibly exacerbating, factor was that Ridgway found and fostered a strong religious aspect to his life. Consistent with his obsessional personality, he took this too to extremes, and again according to Wikipedia he would be "proselytizing door-to-door, reading the Bible aloud at work and at home, and insisting that his (second) wife follow the strict teachings of their pastor. Ridgway would frequently cry after sermons or reading the Bible." Throughout this period, however, he continued his promiscuous and uncontrolled sex life with his wife, girlfriends and prostitutes. It is reasonable to assume this hypocrisy would have further distorted Ridgway's personality, feelings and attitudes towards sex workers.

If he was conflicted by the hypocrisy of being a religious adulterer, and he harboured complex conflicting feelings towards his mother who was herself a prostitute in his eyes, then Ridgway had a strong launch pad for his aggression. Coupled with his abnormally high sex drive and lifelong promiscuity, he would have been a time-bomb of lethal potential. He claimed to have killed up to 75 women. He is known to have killed 49. It is extremely difficult to imagine how this is possible without being caught. It is also difficult to come to terms with the events which followed his capture and conviction.

Once the American media got hold of the story there was an ugly feeding frenzy of publications, articles, books, TV programmes, etc., so that as many people as possible were able to profit from serial killing. Wikipedia has an extensive list of documentaries, films, articles and books on him. I found the sickest entry to be a reference to "artwork" created by artist P Hansen which consists of a picture depicting Ridgway's face composed of nearly 12,000 portraits of his known victims.

This appallingly insensitive and tasteless creation is simply another small addition to the argument that America stands alone as the home of exploitative profiting from serial killing. Significantly, Ridgeway negotiated an agreement with the prosecuting attorney, when he plea bargained successfully not to receive the death penalty in return for providing the authorities with sufficient information to allow them to find as many of the victim's bodies as possible.

Ridgway was subsequently interviewed over the years by various people including Dr Mary Ellen O'Toole, an FBI profiler, who spent many hour trying to get him to open-up about the killings and how he became a serial killer—at that time America's record holder for the most victims. He said: "Sex and hurting women started at an early age." She said he referred to himself at one point as "A lean, keen killing machine." Once, he took his son along with him on a lethal outing, picked-up a woman, drove to one of his pre-selected spots and, in his own words:

> "I took her into an area and my son was there and I killed her. I'm real sure my son didn't see it, but that only happened one time."

Soon after this, when asked if his son had been with him on other occasions, he said, "I didn't want my son to see it again." Now, if he meant what he said, this implies that his son had in fact seen Ridgway kill the woman on the earlier occasion.

O'Toole concluded, "He was a normal, vanilla looking kind of person." And it was true. Ridgway was the sort of innocuous, bland kind of man you wouldn't look at twice and wouldn't remember what he looked like seconds after seeing him. Yet, this blank, insignificant man was one of the worst serial killers in history. He both enjoyed killing women and would have continued indefinitely had DNA-testing not been developed. He was arrested in 1982 and 2001 on charges related to prostitution. He was a suspect in the Green River killings as early as 1983 and hair and saliva samples were taken from him in 1987. But it wasn't until 30 November 2001 that police arrested him on suspicion of murdering four women. What happened in the intervening 18 years since he'd been a suspect and 14 years of police having his DNA samples available to them?

Psychology of a serial killer

So, what is the psychology of this serial killer? Gary Ridgway was influenced in his personality development by his domineering (and possibly inappropriately sexual) mother. His father had worked in a mortuary and is recorded as having told his son stories of both necrophilia and sex workers. He formed a relatively early prejudice against prostitutes, which would have been heightened by his sexual promiscuity, his over-active sex drive, the obsessive demands for intercourse as recounted by his three ex-wives and several ex-girlfriends, his contracting STD from a prostitute, his finding religion in a rather fervent but underdeveloped way while an adult, and his proselytising nature which flowed from it. Also, his success and pleasure on the first occasion when he had sex with and then killed a prostitute, and, crucially, getting away with it. Apart from being a serial killer of prostitutes or women he could illogically persuade himself were promiscuous, Ridgway had no discernible life; and little or no success with women in long-term, equal relationships. The fact that he had, on one known occasion (and possibly more) taken his son with him on his killing outings says a lot about how morally corrupt he was and what an abysmal father too.

I believe Gary Ridgway enjoyed having sex with and killing women. He was quoted by the *Washington Post* saying strangling young women was his "career", and "choking is what I did, and I was pretty good at it." It was easier but not essential that they were prostitutes, both because of his twisted prejudices and that they were, and remain, the "safest" victims to target by virtue of their vulnerability and the low level of societal concern and protection afforded to them.

Incredibly, Ridgway admitted that he had been tempted to kill his mother, his second wife and his third wife. When pressed, he explained that one reason he'd considered killing his second wife was because he didn't want to be labelled "a loser". With typical cynical logic, he didn't pursue these thoughts to kill his "nearest and dearest" from fear that it increased the risk of getting caught.

It is distinctive that Ridgway was able to live a double life so success-fully. No-one who knew him, including his third wife, who was with him for 17-years, apparently had any suspicions. Long-term co-workers and former girlfriends echoed this assessment. It might be said that Ridgway was at least exceptional in his ability to live as both a normal married father and reliable worker, and a cynical, cunning serial killer the likes of which America had never then previously known.

I will leave the last word to Ridgway:

"I wanted to kill as many women I thought were prostitutes as I could."

In that, he was successful. There remain many questions however as to whether there were times during that 18 years when he might have been stopped. True, he was extremely careful, disciplined and cunning . He found early in his killing life that a simple oft-repeated *modus operandi* was the safest. He would cruise along the same road, never venturing too far from home. He disposed of the bodies all along the Green River, which led to his serial killer tag The Green River Killer.

One question however burns brightest. Why did it take from 1987 until 2001 for the crucial DNA-test to be taken when Ridgway had previously been a much-questioned suspect, and whilst DNA-testing had been in place since 1986?

CHAPTER THIRTEEN
TED BUNDY: FOR THE LAST TIME

Ted Bundy: For the Last Time

Why devote any more pages of print to the serial killer that the media and press have gorged on for years? Surely there's nothing new to say about the man who was a 1970s serial murderer, rapist and necrophiliac and was executed by electric chair in Florida in 1989. The only reasons I'm including him is to briefly explain Ted Bundy's psychology, and to highlight the part played by pornography, the mistakes made by police, and the part Bundy himself played in the popularisation in cultural terms of serial killing in America.

For the record, Bundy kidnapped, assaulted, raped, murdered and sometimes he dismembered a total of at least 30 young women. We know this total only because he eventually confessed to it. He was only convicted of three murders, one attempted murder and assault.

Why is Bundy so popular?

The assertion itself, that we are dealing with an issue of "popularity", was confirmed to me when I read an article in the *Sunday Times* magazine entitled "How I fell in love with a serial killer", and it was about Bundy, written by a woman who "fell under the spell of a charming stranger."

What is wrong with us? Where have our consciences gone? I understand that it is possible to be a serial killer and behave as if you aren't, to appear normal and stable as other examples in this book demonstrate. But they aren't normal and stable people. And they do terrible, irredeemable, things. And when that happens, we shouldn't continue to treat them as if they have fallen and can be redeemed by some degree of penitence as in the Christian faith. We need to deal with reality and to condemn what they have done. When numbers of women continue to find Ted Bundy attractive, they need to examine their conscience, quietly and in private.

"Bundymania"

The most extreme example of Bundymania must be that seemingly exhibited Carole Ann Boone. To quote from *Psychology Today*:

> "She moved from Washington State to Florida to be close during Bundy's trials, married him and had his daughter. Boone believed in Bundy's innocence and claimed he was being railroaded. During the penalty phase of his final trial in 1980 she even testified on his behalf."

Stephen Michaud interviewed Boone—and noted that she referred to this killer of 30 women by such affectionate names as "Anglebuns" and "Bunnykins".

Apparently, there were hundreds of young female Bundy fans at the time. This despite the fact that he was convicted in an open court which heard months of evidence confirming his guilt. And he confessed and subsequently helped the police with other cases based on his indisputable guilt and knowledge of serial killing. "These women aren't just behaving irrationally. They are behaving immorally and irresponsibly. The credence they give, and the sick phenomenon of, e.g. Ted Bundy t-shirts and fan clubs, add to the trivialisation of murder and the enhancement of the sick spectacle of celebrity status for the worst among us. Their behaviour is nothing less than shameful."

To my mind there can be nothing but contempt for this phenomenon. Yet it is easily explained. Bundy was handsome, charming, intelligent, said to be "charismatic", and young—and yet he was still a serial killer. If he had not been a serial killer and one who became famous thanks to the American media's obsession with him, he would have remained anonymous and insignificant. Throughout my over 20 years working directly with hundreds of murderers, I have observed this irrational fascination women have for "attractive" killers (including serial killers) first-hand. On many occasions, women would establish a correspondence with these life-sentenced prisoners and many would visit the men, which would become regular and increasingly took on the nature of unconsummated affairs. It was also a relatively common event for official female prison visitors, even those who were married, to be drawn into inappropriately emotional relationships with prisoners. It is women overwhelmingly who are drawn to these monsters, so much so that, perhaps inevitably, an American, Dr John Money, coined the term "hybristophilia" to describe addictive sexual arousal to violence and attach it to the Bundy-generated phenomenon.

For me, this is too narrow a compass. There are other significant factors operating which aren't directly sexual. I posit that many women who have suffered failed relationships where they were the recipient of aggressive, verbal and physically abusive behaviour from men, find safety and security in having a relationship which is safe from direct aggression, and what could be safer than for the man to be serving an indeterminate life sentence in prison? Safe, but with the added frisson that the man himself has an exciting history of rape and/or murder, so the woman can experience the thrill of excitement free of the risk of personal abuse.

I resist the American obsession with finding a psychiatric label to stick on such behaviour as if that explains it. It doesn't. It simply gives a short-hand sticker to the characteristics which have already been exhibited, a kind of circular, false reassurance. Labels such as "anti-social personality disorder", "psychopath" and, now in the immediate context of forming relationships, "hybristophilia", don't explain, they simply label. We can't justify the behaviour of women by labelling their dysfunctional adoration of serial killers, we can only try to understand and, ideally, prevent this.

Commercialisation

The abiding financial appeal of Ted Bundy is even easier to explain and far harder to justify. For the past 45 years, the American media, including news channels, journalistic articles, books, TV programmes, dramas and movies, have feasted on the Bundy story. While there have been many who objected to this frenzy, their objections have come to nought. Such is the paucity of moral integrity in the business of entertainment and the magnitude of power in the profit motive. Crucially, Bundy was white, young, attractive, intelligent, apparently charming, not working-class, and he chose attractive, white, young, predominantly college-based, victims, many of whom seemed to be similar in appearance to the one who had rejected him (see under the next heading). Until Bundy, serial killers had often been obviously unstable or unattractive or both as is well-demonstrated elsewhere in this book.

The psychology of Ted Bundy: "poster boy"

Ted Bundy was inadequate in his relationships with women. His fragile ego strength and latent sexual sadism were triggered by rejection when a woman broke off a relationship because she, and her family, didn't think he was good enough for her or them. He was a narcissist and an egomaniac. He was cunning and calculating and consciously chose to stalk, rape and kill. His primary drive was, as with so many other male serial killers, sex and aggression against women and, in particular, targeting women who represented a group or type which had spurned, rejected, insulted or humiliated the fragile male ego.

My including a chapter, however brief and critical, on Bundy will, I know, be open to the same criticism I have directed towards others who've publicised him. I accept that. My mitigation is that I have included him to illustrate the cultural profit without honour aspect of this topic, and to further illustrate what I believe is a culpability.

I believe that popularising and, in some instances, glorifying for entertainment, serial killers like Bundy actually may increase the risk of other unstable men becoming killers as a means both to the end of becoming famous, and because they grow-up thinking that becoming a dominant, powerful, weapon-possessing, fear-inducing man is better than being an anonymous loser, even if there is a risk of prison or worse. In such minds in criminal American men, the fame is worth the risk. As I said an episode of the TV series *Voice of a Serial Killer*, "Ted Bundy is the poster boy for American serial killing".

CHAPTER FOURTEEN
CONCLUSIONS

Conclusions

The central theme of this book is the argument that aspects of American sub-culture contribute significantly to the number and frequency of serial killers there, and that this explains the fact that over two thirds of all recorded serial killers since 1900 in the world have been American. I strongly suggest this is cause and effect. Before concluding the argument, I would like to make one wider observation concerning human nature.

Human nature

Throughout my research for this book, I have been struck by one fascinating and consistent theme: the human capacity to rationalise away personal culpability; failing to take public responsibility for what people have done or failed to do. Whether it was the witnesses who failed to come forward, the partners who knew or suspected, the authorities or police who failed to act when provided with sufficient evidence, attorneys who defended killers on technicalities when they were obviously guilty, and juries who granted leniency or acquittals which taught potential serial killers they could get away with it. I found no references anywhere to someone admitting their failure in relation to any aspect of a serial killer's development, killing time, or trial. How is that possible?

Most of all, I marvel at the serial killers themselves when they are interviewed. They spend most of the time talking about anything but their killings. They speak of themselves in an obsessively egocentric way. Rarely do we see any sign of contrition or regret. The dominant theme before conviction is denial and self-protection. The dominant theme after conviction is to fuel the obviously insatiable public appetite for perverse entertainment; for safe, vicarious excitement at the expense of personal dignity and decency. I might be criticised for feeding this appetite by writing this book. But at least I have attempted to shed some critical light on the psychology of the killers, the experiences that make them, and review where warranted the failures of the legal system.

Factors to emphasise

I have argued that there are a number of recognisable and understandable factors which contribute in varying degrees and frequency to making a serial killer, including:

- First and foremost, learning that to satisfy your personal, and obviously desperate, need for sex and dominance by means of raping and killing women if you are heterosexual, and men if you are homosexual.
- Being raised in a violent, abusive, dysfunctional or broken home.
- Having an aberrant introduction to sex as a victim.
- Experiencing rejection as intolerable and feeling a sexual failure.
- Failing to form a social conscience.
- Learning to hate those who you perceive as having offended against or rejected you.
- Viewing pornography to obsessive or addictive levels.
- Withdrawing from social contacts.
- Easy and uncontrolled access to weapons, particularly guns.
- Becoming so criminal that killing people is viewed as a means to a profitable, pleasurable or enjoyable end.
- Adopting a rootless or nomadic lifestyle.
- Learning to select victims whose profile significantly reduces risk of capture.
- Benefiting from failures of detection and apprehending at every stage of progression, especially the beginning.

Finally,

- being born and raised in a country where you learn to take your revenge on those who made you what you are by raping and killing innocent others in large numbers.

This list is not comprehensive, but represents what I believe are the main components, or building blocks, in the creation of serial killers.

We have seen illustrated, in the case studies I've provided, compelling individual examples of how these factors contribute to the making of serial killers. We know too that American popular culture is full of promiscuity, pornography, abuse, violence and rootlessness. These occur, I argue, in greater number, frequency, and severity in the USA than in any other country on Earth. And this environment fosters extreme measures to satisfy personal failures, including the extreme of serial killing.

There are, of course, serial killers whose formative experiences don't match this typology. That again is human nature; there are always exceptions to every rule. But from the clinical perspective of someone who has spent his entire professional life working in direct contact with hundreds of murderers and dangerous and severe personality disordered offenders, I believe I know what I'm talking about.

What can be done to address the fact of American serial killing?

Tragically, the obvious answer is, realistically, nothing, or at least nothing short of a major shift in attitudes. I am not so deluded as to imagine this modest book will make a great difference. That policy-makers will be swayed to address this manifestation of a national disease by my brief polemic. Yet, I cannot end without at least trying to make some constructive observations and suggestions if the argument were followed. In an ideal world it should be possible for a dynamic, creative and democratic nation to at least openly and publicly acknowledge the truth that serial killers are a particularly American problem.

I believe the majority of Americans live in a natural state of wilful ignorance concerning the link between serial killing and being raised in the USA. It would be far worse though if I were wrong and Americans accepted the link with indifference or, worse still, pride.

What if I'm wrong and there is no link? How else can we explain the statistics? When I asked the internet why America has the majority of serial killers, I could find no site which even accepts that it is statistically true. Even the author of the research which collected the data, Dr Mike Aamodt, argued that it is because the USA is better at collecting data than other countries so is consequently over-represented. This simply is, at best, a defensive rationalisation. Are we really to believe that technologically sophisticated countries like the UK for example, or indeed most of Europe, are less able to track, record and collate their relatively tiny numbers better than a country as vast and diverse as the USA? Untenable and risible.

Humanism and secular morality

With the continuing, and increasing, decline of the influence of traditional Western Judeo-Christian morality, what is the alternative? The church has, for two thousand years, held sway over the human moral conscience. We were raised to commandments, to prescriptions and proscriptions which carried the ultimate sanction of eternal damnation. It is arguable now that significantly less than half the population of the USA actually believes in, and practices, those religious tenets. Crucially, most of them have replaced Christianity, or other traditional religions, with either atheism or a form of permissive hedonism. People now live their lives believing there are no punishments so long as the act is legal. And many millions act immorally even if it is illegal.

A starting point for stopping the decline of American moral values and behaviour might well be the alternative of Humanism. Briefly, Humanists UK define a humanist as someone who:

> "Trusts to the scientific method when it comes to understanding how the universe works and rejects the ideas of the supernatural (and is therefore an atheist or agnostic).

Makes their ethical decisions based on reason, empathy and a concern for human beings and other sentient animals.

Believes that, in the absence of an afterlife and any discernible purpose to the universe, human beings can act to give their own lives meaning by seeking happiness in this life and helping others to do the same."

An interesting article I discovered on this theme is by Dinant Roode, who describes himself as a "learning engineer", at Hanze University of Applied Sciences in The Netherlands. He has a website article entitled "Education Needs a Humanistic Approach" (see https://dinantroode. com/author/trenducation/). Roode argues that taking a Humanistic approach formally to education and development requires a foundation of core principles: "respect for life and human dignity; equal rights and social justice; respect for cultural diversity; a sense of shared responsibility and a commitment to international solidarity."

These principles could be introduced into classes in American schools as part of an agreed national curriculum. They would go a long way towards addressing the moral chasm left by turning away from traditional religions, the decline in a sense of social and communal collective responsibility and respect, and would be affirmation of the need to "enhance the dignity, capacity and welfare of the human person in relation to others and to nature."

In his closely reasoned article, Roode argues that educational policy needs to move beyond a narrow "utilitarian vision and human capital approach" and expand learning to all it's social, cultural, civic and economic dimensions, concluding with the essential message which goes beyond current American educational thought, of "learning to be and to live together."

Laws against extreme, violent pornography

There is a moral black hole on the internet. I have, as a magistrate, been obliged to view pornography which was evidence in cases before the court. It was dreadful. Image after image, involving children and animals, and I never want to see that kind of material again. Surely it is indisputable that viewing pornography of this type, or any type which portrays people acting with violent impunity, must have a malign influence on formative minds?

It is easy to view videos of pornographic scenes which are legal. Scenes which include rough, aggressive sex and even simulated rape. What happens to the character of young men when they feed on a steady diet of this filth? How does it change their attitudes towards women and sex? It is inconceivable that there is any positive influence. That they might become more sensitive and considerate? No; precisely the opposite. They learn to objectify women and to see them as targets to be demeaned. I have no doubt that this is an essential contributor to the making of a significant number of rapists and, in the most extreme cases, serial killers.

A nationally integrated police computer system for identifying possible serial killing patterns and monitoring them

The FBI has something called CODIS (Combined DNA Index System), a murder and crime activity means of coordination. CODIS has three levels: National, state and local. The report of the "Serial Murder: A Multi-Disciplinary Perspectives for Investigators Conference" held in Texas in 2005, reported that: "When dealing with a serial murder case, investigators need to contact their LDIS or SDIS level representatives … in addition to the NDIS database."

This is the closest thing there is to what is required. It is unclear the extent to which this system would satisfy the needs of police investigators in different jurisdictions to compare and match relevant data on suspect cases which may be linked by the same perpetrator.

I have no expertise in this area, but simply argue that improved chances of acting at earlier stages in the career progression of serial killers would prevent further deaths, and that a better integrated, computer-based network would add significantly to this purpose.

Introduction of new laws addressing parental abuse

USA federal legislation provides guidance to individual states by identifying a minimum set of acts or behaviours that define child abuse and neglect. The federal Child Abuse Prevention and Treatment Act (CAPTA), defines child abuse and neglect as, at a minimum:

> "Any recent act or failure to act on the part of a parent or caretaker which results in death, serious physical or emotional harm, sexual abuse or exploitation"

or

> "An act or failure to act which present an imminent risk of serious harm."

The difficulty is that each of the 50 states is also free to provide their own definitions of maltreatment, and they aren't bound to the federal ones unless they are accepting CAPTA state funding. Also, apparently the CAPTA definition doesn't provide "specific definitions for other types of maltreatment such as physical abuse, neglect or emotional abuse."

It is of course a minefield to consider wider, imposed laws with strong punishments for the diversity and complexity of behaviours which might fall within federal definitions. Libertarians also would express vehement objections to whatever they viewed as infringements of personal liberties.

It is not my intention to suggest that the case is made that there is a proven link between parental abuse and rates of serial killers. Correlation doesn't prove cause and effect. It is only that the presumption of this book is that, if we do nothing, there is every reason to believe that not only will serial killing continue, but that it will increase. And I am personally convinced that being abused and rejected as a child is one of the key experiences in the formative progression towards killing.

This has to be further qualified from the clinical perspective that where the child learns it is better to be the abuser than the abused, and that they have internalised an abiding sense of bitterness and anger from that abuse, then the risk is significantly increased. I must emphasise, finally here, that the vast majority of children who are abused do not go on to kill. I argue rather that the rate of incidence of abuse in serial killers would be far higher than in others.

Introduction of nationally funded courses in social morality

I have argued that there has been a widespread and enduring decline in the levels of interpersonal morality in the USA over recent decades. This has happened partly due to the decline in religious observation and influence, and partly from an increasing permissiveness in the attitudes of people towards sex, fidelity and marriage. A society, or more accurately, sub-cultures, which free themselves from the precepts of moral conduct, and convince themselves that nothing is wrong unless it feels wrong is a culture in decline.

It is difficult to argue realistically for a return to old values such as marital fidelity, especially when some of those in high office so conspicuously set a poor example. There was a time when adultery with prostitutes was held to be beyond the pale for those in public office. That time, in America at least, is seemingly well-past.

Nevertheless, I argue that it is possible and desirable to propose for discussion a national network of centrally funded classes for adults in the ethics and morality of decent interpersonal living. Again, from the position of my polemic about the social formative causes of serial killing, it is possible to argue that the greater the number of consenting adults who have enhanced attitudes about what is right and wrong in how they treat one another the stronger the restraint on the development of feelings of hatred towards others which is a key factor in creating serial killers.

In a personal flight of fancy, would it even be possible for courts to have the option of directing certain particularly anti-social offenders when convicted to attend good citizenship classes. Equally, prisoners who have offended against the person (rather than for profit) might attend similar classes inside prison.

And, finally, introduction of laws limiting the possession of guns, and a national obligation to hand in existing guns in private ownership

I know it will never happen, but the uniquely American obsession with guns is arguably *the* single biggest culturally addictive malignancy there is. It is impossible to reason with gun owners because, as a group, they have the most advanced and entrenched set of delusional rationalisations seen since World War II. Who hasn't heard the specious defence of guns that it is the person not the gun. True, but without the gun, the person is rendered significantly less dangerous, and far less likely to be violent.

Unarmed people find it far more difficult to kill other, unarmed people. I observe, in passing, that the Second Amendment of the American Constitution refers to the prefatory need for a regulated militia and that, therefore, the people have the right to keep and bear arms. Only the National Rifle Association and it's minions would attempt to argue that this justifies tens of millions of Americans holding over 300 million guns including military grade automatic weapons because of the imminent and abiding threat which justifies a standing militia. The USA doesn't have a militia. It has one of the largest professional armies on Earth and the largest expenditure by far in arming them. Militia? Anachronistic and absurd.

The gun is the weapon of choice (even if actually used to kill by a minority) of serial killers. But guns are only part of the psychology of fear which pervades much of the national psyche of the USA. Is it really so unreasonable to argue that there would be significantly less lethal violence if there were significantly fewer guns? At the very least, it could be argued that, where there is a history of criminal convictions for violence, those people should never be allowed to purchase guns of any description. Of course, this too will never happen. And, as a result of the national obsession with firearms thousands of innocent people, many of them children, will continue to die at the hands of those who fail to cope or succeed and take out their revenge on those who do so; the guilty killing the innocent.

In summary

I have come to the end of my limited and admittedly flawed polemic. I believe serial killers are made, not born. I believe further that the overwhelming majority of serial killers are American because of the environment in which they are raised. Further, that this environment isn't just specific abusive families and it's not only a violent culture. The cumulative effect of several endemic aspects of modern American life is to create these "monsters". It is in part the same environment that creates mass-murderers, that imprisons more people than any other country on Earth, that has higher rates of opioid drug addictions and death than any other, that has millions of broken homes, that rejoices in the greatest concentration of pornography sites and viewers in the world, that purveys the maxim "an eye for an eye" to it's sightless conclusion, and it is a landscape where it is possible to disappear from sight for years in a geo-cultural morass.

Of course, these realities exist in other countries, but they do so in far less magnitude and there are many countries which have almost no serial killers. I would argue that this is directly the result of them sustaining traditional familial values, especially through extended families, strong neighbourhood ties, religious sanctions with clear expectations concerning right and wrong ways of living, and because there is no need for people to be so frightened as there is in a country with more guns than people.

As you sow, so shall you reap.

Selected References

Aamodt, Dr Mike (2016), Florida Gulf Coast University Serial Killer Database, Virginia: Radford University.

American Psychiatric Association (2013), *Diagnostic and Statistical Manual of Mental Disorders, IV-R (2000),* Arlington, Virginia: American Psychiatric Association.

Angrilli, A, Sartori, G and Donzella, G (2013), "Cognitive, Emotional and Social Markers of Serial Murdering", *The Clinical Neuropsychologist,* Vol 22, Issue 3.

BBC online (2020), World Prison Populations, International Centre for Prison Studies.

Bogel-Burroughs, N, Williams, T, and Oppel Jr, R A (2019), "How Did a Serial Killer Escape Notice? His Victims Were Vulnerable and Overlooked", *The New York Times.*

Bond, S A (2017), "Psychopathic Killers Hide in Plain Sight", *Psychology Today.*

BBC (2020), World Prison Populations. Online News Channel.

Brean, J (2018), "'I cry all the time': Bernardo denied parole after 25 years in prison", *The National Post,* Ontario.

Conroy, J O (2018), "What makes a serial killer?", *The Guardian,* 10 August 2018.

Cullen, E and Newell, T (1999), *Murderers and Life Imprisonment,* Winchester: Waterside Press.

Dalrymple, T (2010), "Murder Most Academic", *City Journal Magazine,* New York, 28 December.

Edans, J F (2001), "Psychopathy and the Death Penalty: Can the Psychopathy Checklist-Revised Identify Offenders Who Represent 'A Continuing Threat to Society'?", *Journal of Psychiatry & Law,* 29(4): 433-481.

Elliott, M (2015), *The Man in the Monster,* Penguin Press: New York.

Epstein, E (2019), "America is a violent country, with or without guns", *The Washington Times.*

FBI (2018), "VICAP Links Murders to Prolific Serial Killer", Washington DC, United States Department of Justice, November 27, 2018, https://www.fbi.gov/news/stories/vicap-links-murders-to-prolific-serial-killer-112718

Giles, R and Clark, C (2017), *The Face of Evil: The True Story of Serial Killer Robert Black*, London: John Blake Publishing.

Haggerty, K and Ellerbrok, A (2011), "The Social Study of Serial Killers", *Criminal Justice Matters,* Centre for Crime and Justice Studies, Issue 86.

Hallett, N (2018), "Psychiatric Evidence in Diminished Responsibility", *Journal of Criminal Law.*

Harden, B (2009), "The Banality of Gary: A Green River Chiller", *The Washington Post.*

Pullman, L (2020), "Elizabeth Kendall: How I Fell in love with a Serial Killer", *The Sunday Times Magazine.*

Marripedia, Effects of Family Structure on Crime, http://marripedia.org/ effects_of_family_structure_on_crime

Montaldo, C (2020), Profile of Alaska Serial Killer Israel Keyes, https://thoughtco.com

Morton, R J (Ed) (2008), *Serial Murder: Multi-Disciplinary Perspectives for Investigators,* Federal Bureau of Investigation Symposium Report.

Murderpedia, John Wayne Gacy Jr., https://murderpedia.org/male.G/g1/gacy-john-wayne.htm

Murray, J (2017), "The Role of Sexual, Sadistic, and Misogynistic Fantasy in Mass and Serial Killing", *Journal of Deviant Behaviour*, Vol. 38, Issue 7.

Pearlstein, M (2014), *Broken Bonds: What Family Fragmentation means for America's Future,* Rowman and Littlefield.

Ramsland, K (2019), "Girls Who Love Ted Bundy: Why are some young women so disturbingly passionate about this serial killer?", *Psychology Today.*

Roode, D (2016), Education Needs a Humanistic Approach, Trenducation.wordpress.com

Smith, C and Guillen, T (1991), *Search for the Green River Killer*, Penguin Books.

Spiegel, A (2011), Can A Test Really Tell Who's A Psychopath? Npr 24 hour program stream, https://www.npr.org/2011/05/26/136619689/ can-a-test-really-tell-whos-a-psychopath?t=1588763574549

Taylor, A A (2018), America's Bloody History as The Serial Killer Capital of the World, https://www.ranker.com/list/united-states-serial-slayer-capital/april-a-taylor

Turner, Janice (2019), "Porn is warping the minds of a generation", *The Times*, London, June 22.

US Department of Health and Human Services (2020), *Definitions of Child Abuse and Neglect in Federal Law.*

Wansell, G (2011), *The Bus Stop Killer,* Penguin: London, England.

Index

A

abduction *67–71, 83, 103–108, 112–115, 132*

abuse *41, 61, 105*
  child abuse *137, 189*
  family abuse *19*

accountability *52*

Acid Bath Murderer *160*

addiction *31*
  addictive personality *57*

adolescence *43*

adultery *148, 190*

affray *161*

aggression *20, 39, 80, 91, 171, 180*

Alaska *79*

alcohol *18, 31, 43, 162*

alienation *21, 30, 90*
  moral alienation *83*

America *15*

anal insertion *102*

anger *18, 28, 113, 189*

Angulimala *25*

anhedonia *161*

anti-authoritarian *91*

anti-semitism *76*

arrogance *75, 78, 85*

atheism *75*

attachment *42*

avoidance *170*

B

beating *62, 111*

Bellfield, Levi *127–134*

betrayal *26, 42, 65, 139*

biology *51, 63, 118*

bitterness *16, 113, 138, 189*

Black, Robert *101–108*

black women *93*

blame *50, 115, 160*

blunt force *18*

Bradford University *163*

bragging *128, 149*

bravado *160*

broken home *184, 192*

brutality *55, 81*
  in prison *32*

Buddhism *25*

bullying *102, 127*

Bundy, Ted *177–180*
  "Bundymania" *178*

C

celebrity *30, 178*

challenge *75*

charisma *178*

Chicago *61*

chloroform *69*

church *15, 19, 186*

clowns *61, 70, 82*

CODIS *188*

commercialisation *30, 171, 179*

compassion *26, 108*

  false compassion *112, 119*

compulsion *114, 161*

conditioning *40*

Connecticut *112*

conscience *22, 26, 70, 94, 108, 152, 177, 184*

constraints *27*

contempt *78, 80, 120, 148, 160, 170*

contrition *114, 122, 183*

control *42, 85, 108, 140*

  punitive over-control *62*

cowards *111, 165*

  guns and cowards *24*

creed for killing *81*

crime rates *20*

Crossbow Cannibal *159–166*

cruelty *96, 120*

culpability *183*

culture *40, 72, 185*

  counter-culture *75*

  cultural stigma *18*

  culture of violence *23*

  popular culture *142–143, 177*

cunning *65, 180*

D

danger *104, 120, 162*

  in relationships *42*

darkness *82, 163*

  dark fantasies *148*

  dark thoughts *116*

decency *22, 184*

deception *64, 94*

defence mechanisms *94*

defiance *81*

degradation *64, 121, 138*

delusion *29, 79, 143*

  delusional identity *128*

demonology *163*

denial *xii, 94, 94–96, 183*

dependency *31, 32, 57*

depersonalisation *42*

depravity *50, 58, 151*

detachment *49, 161*

  feeling detached *42*

detection *33, 56, 121*

  escaping detection *84*

development *42*

  arrested development *103, 113*

deviance *15, 103, 107*

dignity *184*

diminished responsibility *52*

discrimination *90*

dissociation *96*

  dissociative identity disorder *42*

distancing *30, 67*

distortion *30, 57, 79, 96, 117*

divorce *19, 137, 160*

DNA *39, 93, 172–173*

domination *68, 80, 85, 95, 102, 112*

double life *67, 83, 173*

drama *78*

drive *49, 63*

  subconscious drives *56*

drugs *18, 31, 43, 64, 128, 138, 162*

dual personality *78*

duplicity *64*

dysfunction *57, 160, 169*

dysfunctional lives *83*

E

ego *95, 119, 141, 180, 183*

alter-ego *159–166*

emotion *48, 114*

emotional development *103*

empathy *26, 187*

employment *50*

enjoyment *29, 49, 70, 95, 104, 172*

entertainment *23*

environment *15, 19, 23, 35, 54, 63, 192*

eroticism *78*

erotic urges *118*

escalation *103, 113, 120*

ethics *190*

Europe *17*

excitement *70*

vicarious excitement *184*

excuses *53, 94*

experience *32*

formative experiences *43*

negative experiences *21*

trigger experience. See *trigger event*

exploitation *154*

F

fabrication *94*

failure *95, 111*

police failings *105*

fame *159, 169, 180*

family *19, 116, 149*

fantasy *28, 56, 64, 103, 112, 160*

Federal Bureau of Investigation *16, 172, 188*

fellatio *102*

formative years *19*

fragmentation *19*

Freud, Sigmund *39*

frustration *27, 113*

G

Gacy, John Wayne *61–72*

gagging *111*

gangs *21*

garrotting *68*

gender *45, 143*

gender prejudice *150*

Georgia *91*

glorification *180*

God

"finding God" *117*

gratification *15, 40, 107, 149*

self-gratification *16*

Green River Killer *169*

grievance *30, 44, 143*

Griffiths, Stephen *159–166*

guns *18, 23, 69, 79, 139, 161, 184, 191*

H

hatred *80, 137, 159, 170, 184*

conflicted hatred *70*

hedonism *15, 186*

homosexuality *44, 61, 103*

hostility *20, 95, 148*

pent-up hostility *28*

Humanism *186*

human nature *183*

humiliation *40*, *62*

"hybristophilia" *179*

hypocrisy *171*

I

identity *42*, *63*, *128*

immunity from prosecution *154*

imperatives *39*

impunity *27*, *40*, *102*, *127*, *173*

inadequacy *44*, *114*, *180*

indifference *49*, *94*

inner world. See *reality*

insecurity *128*

instinct *39*

integrity *179*

intelligence *160*

internet *27*, *40*, *187*

isolation *21*, *56*, *80*, *104*, *159*

J

jurisdiction *84*

justification *81*, *141*

K

Keyes, Israel *75–86*

kidnap *92*, *111*

killing machine *172*

knives *160*, *161*

L

lawlessness *127*

learning *44*, *170*, *184*

learned hatred *29*

Leeds University *162*

lesbians *141*

lies *94*

living a lie *78*

Little, Samuel *89–97*

loners *159*

losers *16*, *173*

love *26*, *137*, *139*

M

machismo *70*

malevolence *52*

manipulation *46*, *119*, *150*

marginalisation *29*, *33–34*

mass-murder *23*, *57*, *192*

masturbation *104*, *113*, *120*, *155*

maturation *113*

media *25*, *30*, *55*, *171*

mediocrity *83*

menace *71*, *81*, *162*

mental-illness *16*, *18*, *119*

militarism *25*, *81*

minimalisation *94*, *112*

mitigation *16*, *141*

mood *44*

mood disorder *18*

Moore, Tyra *139*

morality *152*, *186*, *190*

immorality *45–58*

moral absolutes *15*

moral chasm *187*

morbidity *78*, *102*, *160*

mothers *21*, *42*, *43*, *51*

motive/motivation *39*, *49*, *54*, *56*

murder

first murder *66*, *141*, *143*

murder kits *81*

N

narcissism *180*

necrophilia *64, 172*

neglect *22*

nomads *91*

normality *63*

nurturing *21*

O

obfuscation *34*

objectification *49, 56, 107, 112, 170, 188*

obsession *40, 57, 114*

opportunity *54, 56, 58*

outsiders *79*

P

paedophilia *101, 103, 106*

pain *40*

parents *75, 137, 160*

   parental abuse *62*

   parental bonds *20*

patterns of offending *33, 102, 114, 140*

permissiveness *15, 190*

personality

   absence of personality *169*

   personality disorder *x, xi–xii, 18, 46, 53,*
      161, 179, 185

perversion *107*

planning *80, 84*

pleasure *49, 94, 152, 173*

police *26, 33, 69, 84, 188*

   anti-police *127*

   police failings *153*

   police response *90*

   the enemy *22*

pornography *23, 44, 64, 105, 159, 184*

   pervasive pornography *27*

poverty *90*

power *18, 42, 68, 85, 95, 103, 108, 140, 149*

predation *29, 61, 81, 102, 155*

prejudice *75, 173*

premeditation *41, 48, 56, 108, 112*

prison as industry *32*

profit *18, 31, 171, 180, 184*

promiscuity *127, 138, 171*

prostitution *18, 28, 64, 90, 160, 170*

psychiatry *123, 161*

psychology *155, 172, 177*

psychopathy *46, 71, 94, 161*

   schizoid psychopath *161*

psychosis *18, 142*

public face/persona *64–65*

public health *28*

R

Radford University *16*

Rampton Secure Hospital *161*

rape *27, 49, 61, 79, 91, 111, 137, 149*

rationalisation *43, 94, 122, 183*

reality *30, 117, 164*

   derealisation *42*

   disturbed reality *81*

   fantasy to reality *121*

   feeling real *111*

   inner and outer realities *44, 55*

rehearsal *56, 64, 79, 121, 170*

reinforcement *104*

rejection *21, 43, 46, 57, 63, 105, 180, 184*

religion *171*

repressed urges *65*

resentment *44, 113*
  suppressed resentment *116*
responsibility *27, 140, 183*
  personal responsibility *16*
retaliation *113*
retribution *16, 40*
revenge *44, 56, 142*
reward *49, 148*
Ridgway, Gary *169–174*
risk *70, 84, 155, 162*
robbery *91, 137*
rootlessness *95, 184*
Ross, Michael Bruce *111–124*
rule of law *26*

S

sadism *40, 149, 161*
  "sexual sadism" *118*
safeguarding *21*
safety *22, 137*
Satanism *161*
schizophrenia *137*
secrecy *27, 64*
self-abuse *123*
self-defence *39, 66, 137, 140*
self-hatred *45*
self-image *41, 85*
self-indulgence *15*
self-penetration *102*
self-preservation *113*
self-protection *183*
self-worth *43*
serial killers *xi–xii, 55*
  most prolific *89*
sex *18, 25, 39, 80, 85, 95, 111, 180*

early sexual feelings *27*
sexual ambiguity *106*
sexual arousal *81*
sexual drives *63*
sexual fantasies *155*
sexual frustration *27*
sexual identity *63*
shame *30, 65*
shooting *140*
signals *160*
skills *82*
socio-cultural influences *51*
sodomy *62*
stabbing *18, 66*
stability *19, 139, 160*
staging posts *170*
stalking *121, 180*
statistics *17*
strangulation *18, 51, 92, 93, 111, 170*
stress *22*
submission *80*
sympathy *140*

T

tantrums *102*
targets *29, 128, 180*
  easy/safe targets *49*
taunts *79*
testing-out *81, 85*
thrills *66*
torture *81, 151*
trauma *62, 108*
  childhood trauma *42*
trigger event *43, 48, 55, 79, 140, 147*
trivialisation *178*

trust *22, 42, 51*

tyranny *70*

U

urges

"uncontrollable urges" *115*

Utah *169*

V

values *26*

vandalism *102*

Ven Pariah *159*

"vermin" *79*

victims

overlooked *89*

victim selection *115*

vulnerable victims *56*

vindictiveness *141*

violence *19, 23, 43*

as entertainment *23*

domestic violence *61*

voyeurism *113*

vulnerability *41, 56, 70, 89, 128, 164, 173*

W

weapons *83, 161, 184*

wilful ignorance *185*

witnesses *183*

eliminating witnesses *49, 137*

worm within *78*

worthlessness *138*

Wournos, Aileen *137–143*

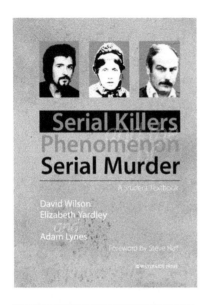

Lightning Source UK Ltd.
Milton Keynes UK
UKHW010658280121
377837UK00004B/651